The Boy They Tried To Hide

Shane Dunphy worked for fifteen years in frontline child protection, in many parts of Ireland. He now teaches social studies and psychology and is a regular contributor to television and radio programmes on issues of child and family welfare. He lives in Wexford with his family.

During his career as a child protection worker and journalist, Shane Dunphy has come into contact with many vulnerable children and adults. The names and details in *The Boy They Tried To Hide* have been changed to protect the privacy of individuals but the events are based on real life events and happenings.

Also by Shane Dunphy
Wednesday's Child
Crying in the Dark (also published as *Last Ditch House*)
Hush Little Baby
The Boy in the Cupboard
Will Mammy Be Coming Back for Me?
Little Boy Lost
The Girl Who Couldn't Smile
The Girl from Yesterday

The Boy They Tried To Hide

SHANE DUNPHY

HACHETTE
BOOKS
IRELAND

First published in Ireland in 2016 by Hachette Books Ireland
First published in paperback in 2016

2

Cataloguing in Publication Data is available from the British Library.

ISBN 978 1 4736 3245 5

Typeset in Arno Pro by Bookends Publishing Services, Dublin
Printed and bound in CPI Group (UK) Ltd, Croydon, CR0 4YY

Hachette Books Ireland policy is to use papers that are natural, renewable and recyclable products and made from wood grown in sustainable forests. The logging and manufacturing processes are expected to conform to the environmental regulations of the country of origin.

Hachette Books Ireland
8 Castlecourt Centre
Castleknock
Dublin 15, Ireland

A division of Hachette UK Ltd
Carmelite House
50 Victoria Embankment
London EC4Y 0DZ

www.hachettebooksireland.ie

For Professor Patricia Casey,
as true a friend as anyone could ask for

SHANE DUNPHY: Do you see many childcare workers?

DR BROWNE: Some, yes.

SD: Have you ever worked with children yourself?

DR B: While at college. I did some work in child and adolescent psychiatry but decided not to specialise in it.

SD: Why?

DR B: I was more interested in working with adults. What attracted you to it?

SD: It is kind of the family business, I suppose.

DR B: Really?

SD: My mother taught children with special needs throughout most of my childhood, and she worked in a residential unit with young offenders before she got married. My dad still works in a community project helping psychiatric patients to reintegrate into society. You could say I was destined to do this kind of work.

DR B: You feel you had no choice in it?

SD: What do your parents do?

DR B: Both doctors.

SD: We are the sum of our parts.

DR B: You could have gone into academia. You didn't have to work at the coalface.

SD: Those who can, do, those who can't, teach. I have been teaching for the past couple of years, actually. See? I'm opening up already.

DR B: Why are you here, Shane?

SD: (*Sighs deeply.*) I think I need help.

DR B: You're in the right place. What kind of help? Tell me about it.

SD: I'm not sure how to begin.

DR B: Wherever you feel comfortable starting.

SD: Okay. [*Pauses.*] I think it all started with something as inoffensive as a walk.

1

The ancient woods stretched for miles in all directions. Some of these trees had seen the Normans arrive in the twelfth century, and the place had a sense of majesty and power. Overhead, rooks croaked and the occasional jay squawked in muted conversation.

George Taylor stopped a few metres ahead of me. He was the principal of St Smoling's – the secondary school in Garshaigh, a small town ten miles west of the forest we were hiking through – and my boss. He was a slim, agile man about fifteen years older than my forty; his grey hair brushed straight back from a slightly domed forehead. Like me, he was dressed in walking gear of neutral colours. A backpack with essentials (water, food, compass) for a trek such as this was slung on his back.

'There's a good spot up ahead to stop for lunch,' he said.

'Great,' I replied. 'Lead on.'

Garshaigh, one of the most westerly towns in Ireland, was surrounded on all sides by woodland, moor and heath. Since coming to live there I had delighted in exploring the local wilderness, a pastime that had found me and my independently minded black greyhound, Millie (who ranged about among the trees as we walked), skirt miles of beach and coastline, work our way up rocky escarpments in the nearby Reeks and learn to navigate wood and forest. I soon discovered that George Taylor was an enthusiastic devotee of the local walks and hikes, and he often accompanied me and Millie on our treks.

I had been living in Garshaigh for two years and was starting to think of it as home. I worked part time at the school as a resource teacher, mostly teaching children with special educational needs, and part time at a local newspaper, covering whatever stories the editor, Robert Chaplin, sent my way. I taught a night class in childcare one evening a week during term time, and over the summer holidays I helped out at a summer camp for kids who wanted to learn about Irish traditional folk music. When I wasn't working, I read, cooked, walked and played at a couple of open sessions in the local pubs. I was happy, relaxed and in good shape, and felt like a wholly different person to the individual who had fled his job working for the social services twenty-four months previously, unable to cope with the sudden death of a close friend and the stress and strain social care was having on his life.

George cut a passage through a bed of bracken, making for what looked like a rabbit path that led to a dense copse of conifers. I whistled for Millie, who had wandered farther away than I was happy with, and made after my friend.

The trees parted slightly before us, revealing a low roofless building, covered in bindweed and sphagnum. George stopped and waited for me and Millie to catch up.

'There's some rocks and deadfall we can use as tables and chairs,' he said, gesturing about. 'It's as good a spot as any and better than most.'

'What was this place?' I asked, unshouldering my pack.

The building, which seemed to be made up of only two small rooms, was in a shallow bowl amid the trees, meaning the location was sheltered and quiet – in fact, as I stopped and took stock of where we were I remember thinking it was like the woods had taken a breath and held it. About the clearing some trees had come down, as George had said, in a recent storm, but none of these had fallen even close to the old building. If I didn't know better, I would have said that it looked like the trunks had put up a kind of protective barrier around the little house – as if something in the forest was encircling it.

'I'm not completely sure,' George said, brushing leaves and bark from a tree stump and beginning to unpack his lunch.

'I don't think I've ever heard you say that before,' I said.

'And you're unlikely to ever again,' he shot back. 'The reason I am unprepared to commit to a hypothesis is that there are conflicting reports on the structure here.'

'A mystery!' I said, sitting down on a large stone. 'Do tell.'

'Well, the most widely held belief is that this is your bog standard woodcutter's cottage, right out of the Brothers Grimm.'

'Is that likely?'

'This woodland was owned by three different local families, and they would have guarded it jealously. You still get deer and pheasant in good numbers, and the trees themselves generated income from more than just their use as firewood; you will find hardwoods like beech here that are excellent for building. I can't imagine those families allowing anyone to impinge on their profits.'

'The other theory then?'

'A lot of people call this the poacher's cabin.'

'That makes sense too,' I said, unwrapping my sandwiches. 'You said there's lots of game.'

'Indeed, and I would agree but for one significant detail.'

'Which is?'

'This is a stone structure. A poacher would have far more likely cobbled together something temporary that could easily be taken down. Poaching is illegal. Remember that during penal times you could be sent to Van Diemen's Land for shooting a few rabbits that didn't belong to you.'

'So no poachers either then?'

'I don't think so.'

'Surely the most obvious explanation is that it was just some kind of storage building for the local foresters. Someone had to husband all these trees and look after the animals and whatnot,' I said.

'I'd concur but for the fact that I checked the old maps of the area. All storage sheds are listed, and this one isn't there.'

'Could be an oversight, or it might have been built after the inventory of buildings was done. Maybe someone local just built it without permission, was evicted, and the structure was left here to rot. Life doesn't always follow neat lines or easy logic.'

'True.' George fumbled in his bag for a moment, and came out with a small bone, wrapped tightly in clingfilm. 'Here you are, Millie.'

He tossed the unwrapped gift onto the forest floor just a few feet from where we were sitting. The dog was perched on a low hillock some ten feet away. When George said her name, she stood up, whined unhappily, then turned around three times and sat back down.

'Odd,' George said. He got up and tossed the bone a little closer to her. She moaned again, clearly upset at something, but would not move.

I realised that she had not come any closer than that point since we arrived. Millie is a coward, and the presence of a badger's sett or fox's den might be enough for her to keep clear. I stood up and went over to her.

'Come on, girl,' I said, catching her by her collar gently. 'Come and join the group.'

Millie looked at me as if she were deeply depressed, and refused to budge a single inch.

'Dogs are funny animals,' George said, placing the bone in front of Millie when it was clear she was not for moving. 'They hear and smell things you and I can't.'

'For most dogs I'd agree,' I said, sitting back on my rock and sipping some coffee. 'With Millie, though, you always have to factor in that she might just be messing with your head.'

'I think you can be very unfair to old Millie,' George said, casting a sympathetic eye towards the greyhound, who in turn gave me a filthy look.

'You should hear what she says about me.'

We finished our lunch and Millie gnawed on her bone from her position on the perimeter. In time we cleared up in readiness to trek on, but as we were about to leave the cottage and its hollow

I paused, suddenly feeling as if every single hair on my body was standing on end.

'Did you hear that?' I hissed at George.

Millie was stock still on her perch, bolt upright, her ears erect.

'Did I hear what?'

I listened intently, more than a little unnerved.

'What did you hear?' George asked again.

I shook my head. The woods seemed to have returned to their usual programme of birdsong and wind-tossed leaves.

'Oh, it was nothing,' I said, unable to suppress a shudder.

'It was enough for you to stop us dead in our tracks.'

'I thought I heard a child crying,' I said, embarrassed now. In my mind I could still hear the wail, forlorn through the trees.

'A child?'

'Yes. Close by. It was just for a second, then it was gone.'

George patted me on the shoulder and moved on.

'Woods are strange places,' he said. 'Let's make tracks.'

We did, Millie disappearing into the trees, rejoining us about half a kilometre farther on, as if she wanted to put as much distance as possible between herself and the ruin.

An hour and a half later we broke from the trees and came out onto a deserted, windswept beach, the breakers crashing in with unrelenting force and great black-backed gulls wheeling above us. We sat on the sand and watched the water and the birds for what seemed like a long time.

Four months would pass before I thought of the lonely, ruined cottage in the depths of the woods again, and by then it was almost too late.

2

Two days later I was sitting at my desk in the offices of *The Western News*, working on an article about the rejuvenation of the local farmers' market, which had been going from strength to strength over the past few years. I tried to do most of my weekly food shopping there and found it a great social occasion also – most of the town turned out, and there were always buskers, street performers and colourful stalls to keep the shopper entertained.

One of the things I relished about Garshaigh was the town's sense of community. Even though I was probably one of the more recent blow-ins, I was still considered (more or less) one of 'them', and this made me feel welcome and appreciated. The market was just another aspect of the many social functions that made the place what it was, and I wanted to write something that would reflect that. I was looking at the selection of photos our in-house lensman had snapped of the previous Saturday's gathering when my mobile rang.

'Yeah.'

There was silence at the end of the line, or at least the sound of an open connection, while the person on the other end decided whether or not to speak.

'Hello,' I said, speaking more sternly this time. 'Can I help you?'

At last: 'Can I speak to Shane Dunphy, please?' It was a male voice, middle-aged, I guessed.

'Speaking.'

'Oh.'

'Who is this, please?'

'My name is Fred Stubbs.'

'Fred Stubbs, editor of *The Clare Voice*?'

The Clare Voice was another small local newspaper. I had met Fred once or twice at industry events and liked him well enough. He had been a journalist his entire adult life and took great pride in providing a service for his community.

'Yes, but this call is personal – sort of. At least, it hasn't anything to do with the paper.'

'Okay. What can I do for you, Fred?'

Another pause followed. I let it hang – I had a feeling he would get to his point (whatever that was) in his own good time.

'Mr Dunphy—'

'Shane, please.'

'Shane … yes, of course. Um – Shane, have you ever heard of a man named Rex Gifford?'

I had an instant feeling of nausea, followed by a short blast of raw, white-knuckle fear, as if someone had just dumped a bucket of icy water over me.

'Yes, I know the name,' I said through gritted teeth.

'Can I ask you how you know him, Shane?'

'Why do you want to know?'

'I want to be sure I am speaking to the right person.'

I sighed deeply and sat back in my chair.

'I have heard of Rex Gifford,' I said deliberately, 'because I am one of the people responsible for putting him in prison three years ago.'

Rex Gifford: five feet and five inches of sickness and guile. An unquestionably brilliant man with an IQ that was off the charts, Gifford was one of the worst serial sex offenders I had ever had the misfortune to encounter. Despite the fact that he held half a dozen degrees, three of them postgraduate, he had made a habit of applying for jobs in cafés, second-hand bookshops, pubs and libraries in the vicinity of colleges around the country, never settling in any location for very long, and leaving behind a trail of traumatised young women too terrified to report what had happened to them.

A dapper, beatnik of a man in his late forties, Gifford's method of operating was well rehearsed: he targeted lonely, isolated girls away from home for the first time, often searching for father figures. He made a point of being friendly and generous with his time, befriending these lost souls with remarkable ease. He would inveigle his way into their confidence, loaning them books, giving them free lunches in his café or ordering rare books for them in the store where he was employed. Sometimes he would offer to help them with their dissertations, wowing them with his knowledge of the complex aspects of their chosen subject, rarely revealing that he was in fact a skilled academic, able to turn his hand to any discipline, it seemed. I wondered, when I first became involved in the case, why Gifford just didn't get a job lecturing in a university – surely that would facilitate even greater access to students. But then I realised: by remaining on the peripheries of academia, he could stay off the radar much more effectively. Gifford was, above all else, a predator, and predators learn instinctively how to blend in.

I first came into contact with Rex Gifford through a young woman named Hayley Porter. Hayley was a brilliant musician, studying for a BA in Performance in one of the colleges in the city where I worked for the Dunleavy Trust, a voluntary organisation that specialised in working with extreme cases of young people in need. Hayley fit this category owing to her quite profound autistic tendencies – she was a superb pianist with a remarkable ear (Hayley could tell you if one of the violins in a large orchestra had a string slightly out of tune) but was absolutely crippled when it came to people. She took almost everything that was said to her literally and struggled with concepts such as humour or simple etiquette. At college she was accompanied by Bridget, a special needs assistant (SNA), who helped her to cope with the day-to-day challenges of classwork and simply getting about the large campus.

One day in March, Hayley's mother received a phone call from Bridget to say she had the flu and could not work that day – possibly not for the rest of the week.

Despite the absence of her SNA, Hayley insisted on going to college and made a point of following to the letter the routine she and her assistant had established, right down to going to the same café for lunch – the café where Rex Gifford had secured a job.

Hayley was a beautiful girl: twenty-one years old, dark hair, brown eyes, slim, with a flawless complexion. She had little concept, however, of her own attractiveness, and anyway, many suitors were put off by her abrupt manner. You did not have to spend much time around Hayley to know that something about her was not quite right.

Rex Gifford had been watching her closely and was far from put off.

Hayley required that her meals be laid out identically each time, with the individual components placed in precisely the same spot on her plate. Usually, her assistant dealt with this, rearranging the food into the required pattern before Hayley saw it. Her teacup had to be filled to just the right place (a mark had been cut into the inside of the utensil to ensure accuracy), and her milk had to be skimmed, not low fat. Gifford had observed these rituals carefully, and, when he served her, was able to replicate them to the letter. On that first day, he was careful to make only a passing comment to Hayley about the fact that she was alone, which was unusual. Hayley, according to witnesses, simply looked at him in response and grabbed her plate to examine it for any unwanted changes. Finding none, she offered Gifford a nervous smile. The SNA, it turned out, had caught a serious viral infection and was unable to return to work for a week – by which time Rex Gifford was taking his lunch break with Hayley, and they had become firm friends.

It was this fact, in particular, that proved the man's almost remarkable skills to me: Hayley was firmly on the autistic spectrum, meaning that she could present an impregnable wall to people she did not know and trust. It could take weeks, or even months, to break down that barrier and be accepted into her world – in the time I worked on her case, I never got through, and I have some skills and experience with people like Hayley. Gifford managed it in a matter of days.

Had he been a beast of a different colour, Rex Gifford might have been a gifted social care worker, but then, as I got to know him and his case history better, I learned that he could also have been a talented animal trainer, a skilled engineer or a green-fingered horticulturalist. There seemed to be little Rex Gifford could not turn his hand to successfully.

By the time Hayley's SNA had returned to work, the girl was asking to be allowed go for cups of coffee, or to the library, or to the bookshop on her own – acts that her parents and teachers saw as huge leaps towards independence. Little did they know the reality of what was going on.

Hayley Porter was found raped and beaten to within an inch of her life one Wednesday afternoon in the alleyway behind the café where Gifford worked. The narrow lane ended in a cul-de-sac, and the attack happened behind a bank of bins that stood at its end, offering cover.

Yet it was still an audacious crime.

Hayley was discovered in broad daylight. Her wails brought her to the attention of passers-by, who could see that this poor girl was hurt and in great distress, but they could not get close enough to see just how badly she was injured, or to elicit so much as her name from her. The paramedics had to restrain and then sedate her when they arrived.

I first laid eyes on Hayley later that day as she lay unconscious in her hospital bed. Her face had been horrifically battered: one eye swollen shut, some of her teeth broken, a deep bite mark sunk into her cheek. I stood appalled, as I always am at the rampant cruelty human beings seem infinitely capable of inflicting on one another.

So engrossed was I in my thoughts, I didn't even notice Rex Gifford coming to stand beside me. I took him for a family member, shook his hand and offered my sympathies. He accepted them, smiled meekly and turned on his heel, passing Hayley's mother on the way out.

It was an act of huge temerity but, in truth, we never would have caught him if he hadn't come to the hospital. Hayley had walled off the experience, and when she regained consciousness she reacted to the little man just the same as she did to anyone else she did not know, as if he did not exist.

Yet he claimed he knew her, and he visited her several times over the five days it took for her physical injuries to recover enough for her to return home. I was touched by his attentiveness at first, as not many had bothered to check on Hayley, and very few of her classmates had even asked after her welfare – her disability had made her very isolated within the community of students – and while they were upset at what had happened, they did not feel it was appropriate to call on her. This all served to make Gifford's presence even more welcome to Hayley's family. I thought he was just a nice bloke who felt sorry for the strange girl who ate lunch in the café where he worked.

The café that she had been found behind.

I mentioned the connection idly to one of the gardaí who were investigating the case, and she did a check on the records of the staff and regular customers. All came back clean of anything other than speeding tickets and one citation for disturbing the peace.

When I spoke to some of the other students in the wake of the attack (it is customary to see if any students need counselling or are distressed when one of their peers has been assaulted) I discovered that this man had either made a thorough nuisance of himself, tormenting certain women, and stalking others to the point of terror, or been the darling of the campus. All of the objects of his attentions were much younger than him, some by three decades, but in the cerebral environs of a university, this did not receive as much comment as it might elsewhere. Two of the women admitted to having entered into consensual sexual relations with him, and while one shrugged and said it was a one-night stand that had come to nothing, the other admitted she'd had a brief fling with him but discontinued it when 'Rex got really intense and scary'. He had threatened her was as much as she would say, but she showed me abusive text messages he had sent her, something he had done several times daily until she had asked a male friend to warn him off.

I passed this information on to the police, who followed up on it, and Rex suddenly became the prime suspect in the case (in reality, there were no other suspects).

DNA testing sealed the deal, and Gifford was sentenced to two years for aggravated sexual assault. During the trial, my contribution was mentioned as having been instrumental in bringing him to justice, and while he started serving this sentence, other charges resulting from the investigation were to be followed up on, many of them coming from the interviews I had carried out with the other students. It was hoped that getting some of the many girls he had tormented in this university alone to speak up about their ordeals might add to Gifford's years of incarceration. And the police were also checking some of his other places of residence.

My lasting memory of Rex Gifford was of him sitting impassively in court as the details of his appalling attack on Hayley Porter were read out. He did not even attempt to hide the smile that played about his lips, as if the cold, legalistic account of his crime was bringing back a pleasing memory.

I was glad to be rid of him and had made no attempt to keep up with the progress of his case. I had got involved only because Hayley's disability had brought her into my remit, and I had no desire to befoul my life by having a monster like Rex Gifford in it any longer than I had to.

But here he was again.

'He's not in prison anymore, Shane,' Fred said.

'I'm genuinely sorry to hear that. How did you come into contact with him?'

'He approached my daughter in a café near her college yesterday. She's studying for her master's so has been going in over the summer to use the library and such. Thanks be to God she sensed something was wrong. She took a picture of him on her phone and I recognised it from news reports I'd seen.'

'Smart girl.'

'She is.'

'Where's she in college?'

'Limerick. She's doing journalism.'

'You must be proud.'

'As Punch.'

'Have you been to the police?'

'Of course. He hasn't committed a crime, or so they tell me,' Stubbs said. 'All he did was ask her about the book she was reading. He hasn't got a job near the university or done anything that's in breach of his parole.'

'Approaching a girl who fits the profile of his previous victims isn't a parole violation?'

'It seems not. She is an adult female – if he were to keep away from them, he'd have to go and live in a monastery.'

We were quiet for a moment, both of us feeling the weight of what we were discussing, and the narrow escape Fred's daughter may have had.

'Why are you calling me, Fred? I'm not involved in child protection anymore. I'm a writer and a teacher now.'

'I thought you might … I dunno … might warn him off. Let him know we're on to him.'

'It might work – I mean, facing him down has worked before. But then, Rex Gifford is not like other people, Fred. He is a predator. A gentle warning may well make him entrench himself more deeply. Or he could move away from your daughter and double his efforts with some other unfortunate. It doesn't solve anything.'

'With respect, Shane, my only real interest is moving his focus from my daughter.'

'I understand that, but even if he were to draw back now, there is nothing to say he won't stalk her secretly, or pop back up again in a year's time. This guy is an unknown quantity.'

'You helped put him away. He might take you seriously.'

I thought about that. I could always go and talk to him, let him know he was being watched.

'I don't like the idea of letting this person back into my life,' I said after a long pause.

'Thank you, Shane. I appreciate it.'

'Thank me when Rex Gifford has disappeared – and stayed disappeared.'

I should have said no. I should have hung up the phone and pretended I had never heard from Fred Stubbs.

Instead, I set in motion a chain of events that threatened to hurt me and those around me whom I cared about.

3

I couldn't go to Limerick that day because I had deadlines to meet for the newspaper, but I promised Fred that I would make the trip the following morning. Summer was drawing to a lazy close, and that evening I popped over to St Smoling's school to catch up on some preparatory work for the ensuing academic year. I worked primarily with children with special educational or behavioural needs, which meant that I was deployed across several different classes throughout the school, something I enjoyed because it gave me a sense of how the little community of teachers and students were faring as a whole.

That particular evening I wanted to go over the list of students I would be working with in the imminent academic year – some I would simply be following as they moved into their new classes; others I would be meeting for the first time. I liked to be as familiar with each of them and their issues (or as many of their issues as had been identified at this stage in their young lives) as I could be before we were thrown together in class.

The old school building was mostly empty, with just a few teachers photocopying test papers or simply tidying last year's detritus from their desks and filing cabinets. I enjoyed the shadowy coolness of the corridors as I made my way to the main office, where George Taylor had left a bundle of files for me to go through. I slung them under my arm and went to the room where I had taught night classes for the past two years. It was the first room I had ever worked in in the school, and I thought of it as 'mine', even though all classes were used by any number of the teachers, and George doggedly insisted that we should not personalise them with posters or ornaments, keeping all spaces as public as possible.

I worked for a couple of hours, then, feeling the beginning of a caffeine-withdrawal headache, went to the staff room to brew some coffee. I had just filled the kettle when I heard a snuffling sound behind me and, turning, found that I was not alone. Sitting on one of the couches that lined one wall of the room, her head in her hands and quietly weeping, was Maura Bellamy, the other resource teacher employed at St Smoling's and therefore my closest colleague.

Maura had a gentle, easy way with the students and I had learned a lot from her in the past year.

I went and sat down next to her without saying anything. We sat there for a while. The kettle finished boiling. I patted the back of her hand gently and, getting up, made a pot of coffee, bringing it and the cups, sugar and milk over to the low table that stood in front of the couch. Maura stayed silent while I poured us both a mug, and then sat forward and added some sugar and a dribble of milk to one.

We drank in silence. Finally I looked at her and said, 'Want to talk about it?'

'No ... yes. I don't know.'

'Okay then,' I said, and had some more coffee.

'Did you know Tim Fox at all?' Maura finally said after a long pause.

'No. Should I?'

'He left school before you came to town, I think,' Maura said, gazing at a point in the middle distance. 'He was a good kid.'

'Student of yours?'

'Yeah. He was the reason I came to work in St Smoling's in the first place. I was employed to work as a special needs assistant with Tim when he was still in primary school, and I followed him here.'

This was not uncommon – educational staff often followed their charges from class to class or even from school to school.

'Since he needed me less, Mr Taylor found other work for me and encouraged me to upgrade my qualifications.'

'George is good like that.'

'He is.'

More silence. Then:

'When Tim left here, he still had very poor literacy skills, but he was skilled with his hands. He got a job at a local garage, and I thought he'd made it – he loved working with cars and it was something he could make a really good living from. People always need decent mechanics, don't they?'

'They certainly do.'

She lapsed into thought again. I drained my cup and poured another.

'I got a call last May,' Maura said. 'Tim had been arrested.'

She was gathering momentum, and I knew she would find her way to the end of the story in her own time.

'It seems that over many months he had built up a collection of parking tickets and had paid none of them. He told me that he knew what they were, but he couldn't read what it said on them about how to pay. He didn't have a credit card, and he was afraid to go to the garda station. He ignored them. I think he had five or six altogether, and the penalties on late payment had built up. His case was eventually brought before a judge, so that Tim could explain what had happened, but he never showed up in court. A letter had been posted to him, but he couldn't or didn't want to read it. This continued for three court hearings, until a bench warrant was enacted, and Tim was arrested. He froze in front of the judge, who gave him a complete bollicking for wasting the court's time and money. The fines he owed by this time came to fifteen hundred euro, and the judge topped it up to two grand because he saw Tim as uncooperative – of course he wasn't, he was just scared! Tim didn't have the money and just started spluttering when asked how he intended to pay.'

I knew what was coming next. But I remained quiet and waited for the inevitable.

'He was sentenced to four months on Salt Island.'

Salt Island was a prison on a tiny chunk of rock a mile off the country's southern coast, where offenders from our part of Ireland were usually sent.

'Were you in court when they handed down the sentence?'

'No. I didn't even know Tim was in trouble. If I'd been there the outcome would have been different.'

I knew she was right. Simply having someone on hand who is coherent enough to make a reasoned argument in your defence is often enough to prevent a harsh sentence, such as the one Tim received. He would have been seen as an uncouth, out-of-control yob in need of a serious rap on the knuckles, rather than as a vulnerable young man deserving support.

'So how'd you find out he was inside?'

'Tim had watched enough TV to know he was entitled to a phone call. He rang the school and begged the secretary to get me. He asked me to tell his mother, and to come and see him as soon as I could.'

'Easier said than done. You have to be on his visitors' list, to begin with.'

'He had no idea about all the hoops that had to be jumped through, but I made the arrangements, for his mother and me, and we got to see him a week later.'

'How was he?'

'Terrible. I don't think I'd ever seen him so afraid. I don't think I'd ever seen anyone so afraid.'

'The Shaker is not for the faint-hearted,' I said, giving the prison the name the prisoners themselves used.

'You've been there?'

'Always as a visitor, thank God, but still.'

'That first time I visited, it was clear someone had given Tim an awful beating. I kicked up a stink, but it didn't do any good. I visited him every chance I got. By the time a couple of weeks had gone by, he seemed to be settling a little – I mean, it was a short sentence, all things considered. He wasn't in with the really dreadful prisoners, so we urged him to just keep his head down and he'd get through.'

'What happened?'

'Last week I received a call telling me that Tim had committed suicide.' She began to weep again.

'I'm very sorry, Maura.'

'I know, I know. Me too. It was just so sudden – I was with him two days before and he was almost ebullient – there was only a month to go. I had him marking the days off on a calendar in his cell.'

'A month is a long time inside. A lot can happen.'

'I know … but something isn't right about it. Tim had a lot to live for. They were keeping his job for him; he and I had talked about him moving to a new flat, how he might decorate it. I was going to take him for some literacy classes – I felt it was really important to make sure this sort of thing didn't happen again.'

'Still, Maura, anything could have gone wrong.'

'I don't believe Tim Fox committed suicide, Shane.'

'You think he was murdered!'

'Yes, I do.'

'Does that make it easier for you to cope with?'

'No. Either way, the end is just as horrible.'

'The likelihood of finding out the truth is practically zero, Maura. I know some people but …'

'We buried him this morning. Do you know who was in attendance? Me, his mother and the priest. Not even the people he worked with bothered to show up.'

'I really do sympathise, but I don't know what is to be gained from pursuing this any further.'

She grabbed my arm and held on tight.

'We failed this young man, Shane. *I* failed him in life. I don't want to fail him in death too. I want to know what happened, and maybe see if we can't prevent it happening again.'

'If we go down this road, Maura, I cannot promise what we'll find. What you learn may haunt you. You won't be able to unknow the things that will float to the surface once I start poking around.'

'I understand.'

I squeezed her hand and stood up.

'I'll make some calls. Talk to some people. If there is something to know that you don't already know, I'll pass it your way.'

She sniffed and wiped her nose absently with a crumpled tissue.

'Thank you, Shane.'

'You might not be thanking me when we're done.'

'That's why I'm thanking you now,' she smiled.

DR B: Why did you offer to help her?

SD: It's what I do.

DR B: No it's not. From what you've told me, you're a journalist and a special needs teacher, just like your mother. There was no onus on you to take on the task either Fred Stubbs or Maura Bellamy requested you carry out. What do you think motivates you to do these things?

SD: Maybe I felt … responsible for Gifford being loose again.

DR B: How? You have no authority over how the prison system does its business. You were instrumental in having him prosecuted, so it would seem reasonable to say you *saved* a lot of women from being hurt, not that you are in any way complicit in his being at large again.

SD: I walked away from it, though. I felt sick to my stomach even being around him, and I just let it go. I never even checked in on Hayley again.

DR B: Do you keep in touch with every client you encounter through your work?

SD: No. Not all.

DR B: Most of them?

SD: No.

DR B: In actuality, it's very few, isn't it?

SD: Yes.

DR B: So stop beating yourself up and be sensible. Why did you offer to look into this young man's case? As you have already pointed out, it doesn't look like there could be any happy ending or any real closure for your friend.

SD: I thought it would mean a couple of phone calls, maybe a trip to the city, to clear it up. I like Maura. I thought I could do this for her.

DR B: The knight in shining armour riding in to help the damsel in distress.

SD: Something like that, maybe.

DR B: What do you think these ... um ... these people in need represent for you.

SD: They're my friends.

DR B: And yet you just told me you barely knew Fred Stubbs, and you have never met his daughter.

(*There is a long pause.*)

4

The next day brought one of those beautiful golden mornings that come all too seldom in late summer – clear blue skies, a gentle breeze and the air full of birdsong.

My beloved 1981 Austin Allegro Series 3 had finally, after many years of service, died the previous spring, and, despite much soul-searching, I knew there was only one sensible thing to do: I sold it to a local dealer who gave it pride of place as a display item in his showroom – it would never speed down the highways and byways again (in fact, it was unlikely to move without being pushed or towed) but it had a purpose and was the object of much conversation and admiration.

I very much wanted to go for another vintage model (modern cars have always struck me as being a bit soulless) but I was determined not to make a rush purchase – a rebound buy, if you like – so I settled on a five-year-old Skoda Superb to tide me over.

The drive to Limerick took about an hour. I passed the first twenty minutes or so listening to a morning talk show on the radio, but my mind soon turned to the conversation of the previous evening, and using my new car's hands-free capabilities I dialled a friend I thought might help.

'Speak,' came the monosyllabic answer when the call was picked up after only one ring.

'Karl, how are you?'

'I'm very well,' Karl Devereux said. He was an old colleague of mine, a former criminal who had reformed and was currently working on a voluntary basis as a youth and community worker in some very tough parts of the city. Many professionals gave him a wide berth because he seemed to carry an aura of latent, repressed violence, but I had always found him to be a decent, caring man who wanted to atone for the harm he had done in his earlier life.

'I could do with some help,' I said.

'Couldn't you always? I don't hear from you for six months, and now here you are, as usual, making demands.'

'I know. I'm a terrible friend. I'll send you a bouquet of flowers.'

'Make it a bottle of scotch and I might give you a leg up.'

'Done. Now, will you shut up for a moment and listen?'

'Tell me your troubles,' Karl said, and I did, recounting what Maura had said to me in the staff room.

'And your colleague thinks there may have been foul play,' he said when the tale was done.

'She does.'

'And how will knowing the truth help her to sleep better?'

'I put that to her.'

'Knowing more about the kind of life her former student was

forced to endure on The Shaker will only make her more unhappy. It is not a place people should have to live, in my opinion, no matter what crimes they have committed.'

'I agree with you, for what it's worth, but she is determined, and I want to help her if I can. Can you ask around? I'm sure you know someone who can tell you a little about how this kid served his time – did he adjust okay, did he make friends, did he keep his head down?'

'I can ask. You know, though, as well as I do that if there was a nefarious aspect to Tim Fox's death, the criminal community will just close ranks. So will the gaolers – they have chalked it up as a neat, tidy suicide. They won't want to overturn that verdict.'

'We've had to deal with walls of silence before, Karl. Find out what you can. Your scotch is in the mail.'

'It had better be.'

Fred Stubbs had given me directions to the café his daughter frequented, the place where Rex Gifford had approached her. I found parking nearby and, with a copy of Larry McMurtry's *Lonesome Dove* loaded onto my ebook reader, ordered black coffee and a Danish and took a table near the window.

The foot traffic was lighter than I'd expected, but then I remembered that it was still the holidays, albeit the tail end of them. Some summer courses were running in the university, which was situated nearby, and of course postgrads in the middle of research theses were still using the library facilities, which was exactly why Fred's daughter happened to be about when she encountered Gifford. I settled back, sipped my coffee and kind of half-read my book, all the time keeping an eye on the window and those approaching up the street.

An hour later the coffee was gone, the Danish reduced to crumbs, and I had read the same page more than a dozen times without actually retaining any of its content. I ordered another mug, went to the bathroom, and then resumed my post.

Another hour passed with no sign of Gifford, and I was beginning to garner some odd looks from the café's staff, so I paid my bill and wandered up and down the street a few times, keeping an eye on the door of the café.

I was about to write the exercise off as fruitless when it occurred to me that the thoroughfare was lined with coffee houses and eateries, and thought it not unreasonable that Gifford might well be a regular visitor to any of them, so I spent the next forty-five minutes checking to see if my target was in evidence in these other venues, but this, too, yielded no joy. Frustrated and thinking that I would have to try again another day, I returned to my first port of call, which, as it happened, was the last coffee house on the street, to buy a bottle of water for the trip home. I was turning to leave when Rex Gifford walked in the door and stopped dead, his eyes locked on mine.

He had not changed one iota: his hair had no more grey than before, he was about the same weight, his style of dress was identical – today he wore loose plum cord trousers and a Jimi Hendrix tee-shirt, over which he sported a green tweed waistcoat; the ensemble was finished with brown leather sandals and no socks. A khaki backpack hung from his left shoulder. He seemed shorter than I remembered him, but that was probably just a trick of my memory. His height had nothing to do with the potency of the threat he posed.

'Shane Dunphy,' he said, extending his hand. 'It's been a while.'

I ignored his attempt to shake hands and made a sort of grimacing smile instead.

'Rex Gifford. I'll give you credit for not pretending you don't remember me.'

'I am aware that would be the most common tactic of people in my position, but I do not deny my past. I have made mistakes and I have paid for them.'

The hand remained poised before me, but I walked around him and sat back in my old place by the window.

'Join me,' I said. 'We're due a talk, I think.'

Gifford shrugged, went to the counter to order a soy latte and then sat in the chair opposite me, taking a long draught of the milky concoction.

'And what, pray, do we have to talk about, Shane?'

'When did you get out, Rex?'

'Six weeks ago.'

'Diminished time for good behaviour?'

'Indeed. Prison life offered me ample opportunity to do good. I set up a teaching programme, I updated the systems in the prison library. Do you know I even persuaded one of the more disturbed chaps to do the right thing when he had taken one of the guards hostage – he was going to do some rather nasty things to the poor fellow, but I was able to reason with him.'

'Sounds like you made yourself quite useful on the inside.'

'Well, you know what they say: if life gives you lemons, make lemonade. I like to think I'm an adaptable sort.'

'You were, presumably, in a segregated wing mostly with other sex offenders.'

'Mostly. You know that people with my ... um ... *predilections* can have a tough time among the general prison population. The other inmates like to vent some of their aggressions on us.'

'How unfair of them.'

'Oh, they would probably call it honour among thieves, but I think we both know that it just makes people feel better to point the finger at someone else and say we are worse human beings than they are. All stuff and nonsense. Any action is only as bad as the accepted wisdom declares it to be. And opinion is extremely changeable.'

'Opinion on predatory sex crimes is pretty constant.'

'That is a remarkably inaccurate statement for a sociologist. Need I mention the Greeks, the Romans, child brides in Asia? I could continue. Sexuality is something there is little agreement on among societies even today.'

He was trying to bait me, but I was determined not to rise to it.

'Don't you think that locating in a college town is likely to draw problems down on yourself?' I said instead.

Gifford shrugged. 'I'm a long way away from the location of the crime I was imprisoned for. There are very few towns in Ireland now that don't have colleges of one kind or another, and it would be foolish to insist that I stay fifty yards away from every single student in the country. That, my dear chap, would be impossible.'

'Steering clear of student bars, cafés and the near vicinity of a large university, however, would not be so difficult. And yet here you are. Approaching female students.'

Gifford winked at me.

'I simply asked her what she was reading.'

I blinked stupidly for a moment.

'I presume you are talking about the Stubbs girl,' he continued.

'I just asked her about her book. We were in the queue at the cash register – I was only making conversation.'

I realised there was little to be gained from pursuing this. Gifford was beginning to make me very uncomfortable. I felt as if he had far more cards in his hand than I had. I cut to the chase.

'You're on the sex offenders register, Rex.'

'Sadly, yes.'

'You are aware that that fact places restrictions on your behaviour.'

'Of course.'

'If I hear so much as a whisper that you have stepped over any of the lines laid down in your conditions of release, I will make sure you are returned to a prison cell with all your twisted friends before you even know what has happened.'

Gifford shook his head, sat back and took a sip of his coffee.

'How, pray tell, are you going to do that, Shane?'

'All you need to worry about is that I will do it.'

'Really? As I understand things, your career has reached something of a cul-de-sac. Am I incorrect in saying that you are now a journalist for a scruffy little local newspaper? I don't think that gives you very much authority in matters such as this.'

He had checked up on me! I knew then that I was being played. I had no idea how Gifford had done it, and I was unclear as to what exactly he wanted (beyond messing with my head), but I knew for certain that I was sitting in that café because Rex Gifford wanted me to be there. I realised in an instant that I wanted to get away from this poisonous man immediately.

'You don't know anything about me, Gifford,' I said, trying to keep the tremble out of my voice. 'Just because I don't work in social care full time right now doesn't mean I'm not involved at all anymore. I know people who could make your life very uncomfortable.'

'Really? Why aren't they here then? Why come all the way from your idyllic little town to warn me off without anything to back up your allegations? No, Shane my boy, I think we find ourselves in a very different situation today than when we last locked horns. Your threats are meaningless.'

'I don't do threats,' I said, standing up. 'If you come to my attention one more time, I will make sure you go right back where you belong.'

I tried not to run from the café, but by the time I got back to my car I was shaking.

5

At eight that evening I was sitting in the little square of concrete at the back of my small house, playing the mandocello and drinking a beer. I had planted some herbs and wild flowers in pots and placed them about the area to make it seem like a garden, rather than a stretch of carpark someone had forgotten, and it was now a pleasant enough spot to hang out in.

Millie sat in a patch of shade, trying her best to ignore my musical meanderings but unable to resist the desire to throw me looks of disgust every now and then. I ignored her and played on anyway. I thought I might go mad if I didn't.

My choice that particular evening was a traditional reel called 'Fahy's' (named after its composer, the great Galway fiddler Paddy Fahy) which I loved. I always found something new and surprising in it, and the act of making my fingers dance about the notes became a kind of meditation. Mental stillness was what was required just then.

I had been deeply unnerved by my encounter with Rex Gifford and had no idea what to do about him. I had called Fred Stubbs on my way home and told him that I had met with the deviant, but could not vouch for how effective our conversation had been. I admitted outright that Gifford denied any ill intent towards Stubbs's daughter and had simply spent the time we were together trying to intimidate me.

'I may well have made things worse,' I said. 'It was a little like dumping some freshly butchered meat into shark-infested waters. I only hope he doesn't go into a frenzy.'

'You told him you were prepared to go to the cops though?'

'He is in no doubt about that, although it didn't appear to worry him.'

Stubbs thanked me anyway and seemed so sure that my visit had done some good that my own mood almost lifted – maybe Gifford *was* all bluster and perhaps I *had* put him on his guard.

But my mind wouldn't settle; thoughts were running through it feverishly.

The fact that Gifford knew where I lived and worked bothered me, and I was annoyed that I hadn't been more confrontational with him. If I had grabbed him by the scruff of the neck and dragged him outside, informing him that I would give him the hiding of a lifetime if he so much as looked sideways at me or anyone I knew, perhaps his smugness would have dissipated.

I had wanted to – despite being afraid (I would be lying if I said the man didn't scare me). I had felt a great surge of anger at this new invasion of my life. The thoughts of him prying into my affairs, setting me up in the way he had made me want to throttle him. But I doubted that my show of bravado had fooled him. Gifford had made a career out of gauging people's reactions, body language and tones of voice. He was as much an expert in the codes and patterns of human interaction as any psychologist – it was another aspect of his character that made him such a formidable foe.

As I played, my thoughts started to become clearer.

Was Rex Gifford a genuine threat to me? Would he want to declare war on someone who had successfully put him behind bars and still had the resources to place a great many barriers in his path? He was arrogant and self-serving, but he was also a survivor and unlikely to want to place himself in harm's way. I reckoned that I was just too big and aggressive a prey for him to risk going up against. He was probably just posturing, making himself feel like an alpha dog in his new territory.

But that was another thing that nagged at me: why choose that location at all? Why put himself near one of the people who had done him so much damage? For this, perhaps the most pertinent of questions, I had no sensible answer. It could have been a coincidence that Gifford happened to move to a place near me on his release. It could be a simple accident that he had approached the daughter of a colleague, for ill reasons or good. Yet he knew who she was, a voice deep inside reminded me. And that meant he also knew her tenuous connection to me.

The truth was that I didn't believe in coincidences.

I stopped playing and drank some beer, deciding to push the matter from my mind and hope that Rex Gifford would disappear down whatever hole he generally inhabited.

I played on as my dog slept near me and the sun began to drop below the horizon.

It was one of the last moments of peace I was to experience for some time.

6

Karl Devereux called me two days later.

'I never got the scotch,' he said.

'Goddam postal service. I wrapped it pretty tightly – they must have recognised the shape of the bottle and confiscated it.'

'You don't say? I have been asking around about Tim Fox.'

'And?'

'I've made contact with someone who knew him inside.'

'Great. Is this someone reliable?'

'We are talking about a career criminal, Shane. I wouldn't trust this man to look after my life savings, but I think he can be relied upon to tell us a reasonable facsimile of the truth in this particular instance.'

Having spent quite a number of years in prison himself, Devereux's speech was always formal and clipped – he had lived in an environment where a misplaced word could be a matter of life and death.

'Can you come up to the city to meet him?' he asked.

'If you think it will help.'

'Meet me at the Blackalley Community Centre. I'll ask our friend to come there to talk to us.'

'See you soon.'

I packed an overnight bag and rang George Taylor to ask if he would take Millie for a couple of days. Then I hit the road, secretly pleased to be leaving Garshaigh and Rex Gifford behind; his proximity seemed to leave a shadow hanging over the town and surrounding countryside. I felt a weight lifting from my shoulders as I put some distance between us.

Devereux was about six feet tall, slim and well groomed, and dressed in a soft leather jacket, an open-necked white shirt and dark jeans. His brown hair was peppered with grey and brushed back from his forehead; his eyes a pale, cold blue; his face clean-shaven and hard with prominent cheekbones. He met me at the door of the community centre from which he worked. Despite his voluntary status, the Community Development Project in Blackalley, the area where Devereux had grown up, decided to offer him some office space in their building as a mark of respect for all the positive work he had done.

'Shane, it's good to see you.'

I handed him a bottle of twelve-year-old scotch whiskey.

'As promised.'

'We can have some of this later. Our first appointment is inside waiting.'

Devereux's office was a small room with a desk and three chairs.

There were no photos or knick-knacks, not even a filing cabinet. This suited the man down to the ground, because he was intensely private. I had known him for years but had never been to his home, had never met any of his family or friends. I knew as much about Karl Devereux as he chose to tell me, and had enough sense to be satisfied with that.

Sitting in one of the chairs was a man of tremendous height and girth, sporting a massive head and face of grey-white hair.

'Shane, this is Monty Drew,' Devereux said.

I shook the huge man's hand, then Karl and I sat.

'You want to know about young Timmy Fox,' Drew said without preamble.

'Please. I work with a woman who taught him for many years, and she has asked me to find out about his time on The Shaker.'

'I wasn't there when he took his life,' Drew said. 'I'd been moved to the pre-release block. But we were cellmates for most of his time in that shit heap.'

'Did he find it easy there?'

Drew cast me a swift glance before averting his eyes again.

'Nobody finds The Shaker easy,' he said bitterly. 'It's like the worst place you can imagine. I didn't meet him until he'd been in there for a week – they put you in a kind of holdin' tank before you get assigned a cell – but when he did get put in with me, he was still cryin' himself to sleep every night. He was fairly beat up lookin' – someone had prob'ly gotten sick of his whingein' and given him a few smacks. It happens. It's not right, but it happens.'

'How long did it take him to settle in?' Devereux asked.

'Well, I has a rule when I'm inside – I keep to myself. I left him alone for the first few days he was with me. It was obvious that he was only a kid, and this was his first time in pokey and it had all come as a real big shock to him. He just wasn't prepared. You know that look, don't you? That look where they think they're in a nightmare and if they try real hard, they'll wake up and it'll all be over?'

Devereux nodded in recognition. He knew the look alright.

'He had that. For decent folks, that expression is a sign to just leave them poor souls alone 'til they can get their heads around their new situation. For others, though – well, it's like a siren only they can hear, and it drives 'em crazy. Timmy attracted a lot of attention from those types.'

'He got picked on?'

Drew laughed dryly.

'You could call it that, yeah.'

'What would you call it?'

'Explain it to him, Monty,' Devereux said. 'He's alright.'

Drew nodded and took a deep breath.

'He got beat up a lot. And not gentle. I mean he took a severe hammering. They… uh … they fucked with him a lot, too.'

'Fucked with him?' I asked.

'He got molested a lot. Not always raped, in the strict sense of the word, but he had to give a lot of blow jobs.'

I winced.

'I'm a criminal,' Drew continued. 'I'm not gonna deny my past – fuck it, it's probably gonna be my future too; I ain't got no plans to go straight. But when I say I'm a criminal, that don't mean I'm a violent man. I know some of the stuff I've pulled has hurt people, upsettin' them, but I've always tried to target people who could afford to take the hit more or less, and I *never* used a weapon or put no one in the hospital. I'm big, I know that, and that makes people think I'm a fighter, but I'm really not.

'As I watched what them savages was doin' to Timmy Fox, I kind of got mad. Mad like I haven't been before or since. It reminded me of a dog that's been kicked and beat on too much – he lay awake all night whimperin' and talkin' to himself. He was drivin' me mental tryin' to live in the same cell as 'im, but it was more than that. I couldn't live with *myself* sittin' back and lettin' him go through that torment. Prison can take a lot away from you, see, but if you let it take your human decency, well, you've let the bastards win, haven't you?'

'Did you help him?'

'Didn't see as I had much choice. One mornin' a bunch of them came at Timmy in the yard. He hadn't done anythin' to warrant it. He was just standin' mindin' his own business. This one scumbag, they called him Ballsack, he walks right up to him with his cronies and says: *I'm kinda horny this mornin', Tim boy. Reckon I could use the services of that girlish mouth o' yours.* Then he punches Tim right in the gut, brings 'im to his knees. Well, I was over there before I knew that I'd even moved. Ballsack didn't know me. He'd seen me around – s'pose I'm hard to miss. Well, I pushed him aside and told him, calm and friendly like, to leave the lad alone.'

Drew paused.

'He looked at me and y'know, I couldn't tell what he was thinkin'. I guess he was sizin' me up. He wasn't exactly no small piece o' work 'imself, but I figure he was tryin' to work out whether it was worth the risk of takin' me on.'

'He had his mates with him though,' I said. 'You were outnumbered.'

'True, but in prison fights, a lot gets decided in the first couple of seconds. Ballsack knew that I could fairly easily break his jaw and a couple of ribs within the openin' moments of the brawl. His sidekicks might pile in, but by then he'd already be lookin' at a month of eatin' his meals through a straw.'

'So he backed down?'

'He did that time. They came to the cell two days later – not him, but two of his real psycho buddies. They had a knife they'd made out of a toothbrush and a razor blade. I thought poor Tim was goin' to shit himself. I had to hurt those boys pretty bad. Didn't bother me too much. They had it comin'.'

'Tim was okay after that?'

'Word got out that he was under my protection. They left him alone.'

'So you and he became friends?'

'Not right away. He'd been badly messed up – his body and his head. Him 'n' me, after a day or so of companionable silence, we started to talk. Just a little at first, like as if he had to learn how to speak all over again, and he was just tryin' it on for size. But pretty soon it got so he started talkin' when he woke up, and he'd still be goin' when we laid down to sleep.'

'What did he talk about?'

'What din't he talk about? I heard all about his mammy and his teachers and his job in the garage. He tole me how he got in such bad trouble without even knowin' he'd done anythin' wrong. I felt bad for him – if he'd had a half-decent lawyer, he wouldn't ever have been on The Shaker, dodgin' scummers in the first place. I reckon I went on to him about a lotta my stuff too – things I ain't gonna rehash here, no offence meant to you gentlemen. I would have to say I got right fond of the lad. He had a good heart, and he wasn't no coward. A coward would have gone mad with the kind of beatin's he'd got. He bounced back from it. You have to admire that.'

'How was he when you were moved?'

'He was upset. I was too. I felt like I was leavin' a member of my family, we'd got that close.'

'He was doing well though?'

'I wouldn't go so far as to say he was happy, but he was getting through his time and he was as cheerful as a man can be in that place.'

'Did you hear anything about his death?'

'Not until Devereux there told me today. I'm not gonna lie to you – I'm hurtin'. Timmy should be out now, gettin' on with that job he loved. He was too good for that place, and it just et him up.'

I nodded. I knew this giant of a man was telling the truth, tears glistening in his eyes as he recalled his relationship with Tim Fox, a kid I had never met. I could tell there had been a bond between them I might never be able to grasp.

'Do you think he killed himself?'

'I don't know,' Drew said, wiping his eyes.

'Make a considered guess,' I said gently. 'You were gone – his protector. Might ... um ... Ballsack and his buddies have come back for him?'

'I'd asked a friend o' mine to watch out for him.'

'Someone who was able to?' Devereux asked. 'People can be bought off, intimidated. Are you sure your replacement was up to the job?'

Drew lowered his eyes again.

'There wasn't anyone else I could ask,' he said, his voice barely audible.

'Who?' Devereux said, his tone level but firm.

'It was Bob Stills,' Drew said.

Devereux narrowed his eyes.

'Stills was inside with you?'

'You know this guy?' I asked.

'He was a competitor of mine back in the old days,' Devereux said, referring to his time as a professional leg-breaker and explosives expert for the criminal underworld.

'So he would have been capable of keeping any interlopers at bay,' I said.

'He is a lethal individual,' Devereux said, 'but a complete mercenary. He could be dissuaded from his task with the offer of a pack of cigarettes and a Mars bar.'

'I told him that if he saw the young lad safe, I'd look after him when he got out,' Drew said.

'I'm afraid his immediate needs might have gotten the better of him,' Devereux said as he stood up. 'Thank you, Monty. I think we have learned all we can from you.'

Drew rose, towering over Karl and me. He was also wider than both of us put together.

'You'll do that thing for me, Devereux,' he said, clearly still upset. 'That thing you said?'

'I'll have a chat with your parole officer. Although how much good that will do, I cannot say. You shouldn't leave town without giving due notice. But I'll plead your case.'

'I appreciate it,' Drew said, and squeezed out the door.

'Leave it with me,' Devereux said, and the huge man was gone.

We sat back down, and Devereux produced two glasses from a drawer in his desk and poured us both a dram from the bottle I'd brought.

'Thoughts?' he said, savouring the liquor.

'I think he was wholly believable,' I said. 'It looks like he did his best to look after Tim, and when he had to return to his freedom, which is kind of an occupational hazard in prison, he tried to leave the kid in the care of someone he knew could protect him.'

'And despite his efforts, he chose badly.'

'Is it possible this Stills bloke really did keep his word?'

Devereux shrugged. 'He is not a man of honour.'

'Is he still inside?'

Devereux pulled over the phone on his desk and dialled a number from memory.

'Harry? Yes, it's me. Listen, is Bob Stills currently a guest of the state out on Salt Island?' Pause. 'Yeah? Thanks, Harry. Goodbye.'

He placed the receiver back in its cradle.

'He still has six months to serve.'

I drained my glass.

'Can you get us in to see him?'

'Not today. But tomorrow, yes.'

We had another glass in silence as the sun began to set over the city I had once called home.

7

Salt Island is a tiny chunk of rock that sits out in treacherous currents of the city's harbour. An old military fort, it can be accessed only by a small boat that makes the crossing twice daily, once in the morning and again in the evening, to bring a change of guards and the food and other supplies needed to keep the population in reasonable health.

The following morning Devereux and I stood on the deck of the little craft and watched the grey smudge on the horizon getting larger and larger. It was a beautiful day, the sun shimmering on the green water as we chugged towards the Victorian edifice. I don't like prisons – they cause me to suffer a mild form of panic attack, probably some innate fear of being closed in. Strangely, Devereux, who had actually been on the inside and experienced all its horrors, seemed quite calm.

'Does it ever bother you, coming out here?' I asked him.

'Should it?'

'I dunno – I've never been locked up and it bothers me.'

'You haven't had to face that fear. I've always thought that a lot of the anxieties we have are really about the unknown.'

'You don't need to have been in prison to know that it's horrible.'

'True. But perhaps it's about gradations of horror. I know just how unpleasant it is, and know that I can deal with it.

Bob Stills was not what I had expected. He was perhaps fifty years old, balding, what was left of his hair greased back flat against his scalp. He was shorter than my five feet nine inches and had a pronounced beer belly pushing against his prison uniform. He greeted Devereux warmly.

'Karl, good to see you my man. How's life on the straight and narrow?'

'To my great surprise it is suiting me very well,' Devereux said, actually smiling (a rare thing).

'And who is your friend?'

We shook hands.

'This is an associate of mine, Shane Dunphy. He has asked for my assistance on a fact-finding mission.'

'Sounds intriguing,' Stills said, leaning in confidentially.

'We have heard that a young man named Tim Fox was placed under your protection a little while back,' I said.

Stills' entire demeanour changed, his 'hail-fellow-well-met' attitude rapidly becoming defensive and sour.

'Now, Karl, you know how it is in this place!' he said, anger invading the edges of his speech.

'Bob, settle yourself down,' Devereux said, patting the man gently on the arm. 'We have not come to make things unpleasant for you. All we want to know is what happened to the lad. Shane here teaches in the school he used to attend, and one of the staff there was fond of him and is a little upset at his untimely end. We thought you might be well placed to fill us in on what happened.'

'That's where you're wrong,' Stills said, sitting back and casting a glance around the visitors' room to see if anyone had noticed his minor outburst. 'I wish I could help you, but I can't.'

'That seems inhospitable,' Devereux said coldly. 'Shane here has come a long way to visit.'

Stills sighed deeply – I could see he was very agitated now and finding it hard to control his temper.

'It's not that I don't want to – I *can't* help you.'

'Why?' Devereux shot back.

'Because I was in the fuckin' hole when he died.'

'The hole' is prison slang for solitary confinement, isolating a prisoner who has behaved badly: been violent or abusive to a fellow inmate or a guard, for example. It is a controversial method of controlling behaviour, since it can have severe psychological effects, but it remains a regular feature of prison life in most parts of the world.

'He was alive before you went in?' Devereux asked.

'He was happy and healthy, all excited about gettin' out in a few weeks. He could be an annoyin' little fucker, but he wasn't a bad kid. I put the word out that if anyone laid a finger on him while I was out of circulation, there'd be serious fuckin' retribution when I got out.'

'What did you go down for?' Devereux asked.

'They found a mobile phone I'd had smuggled in. It was a random cell search – I'd gotten sloppy and hadn't hidden it as well as I should.'

'You weren't set up? No one squealed on you?' I asked.

'Naw. I thought about that, but it didn't make sense. It was just a dumb fuckin' mistake. They were really lookin' for smack in the cell beside mine – only turned me over to make it look random.'

I shook my head. Fate had conspired to make Tim Fox's time on The Shaker exceedingly harsh, it seemed.

'What did you hear when you did get back to general population?' Devereux asked.

'Just that he'd topped himself, taken an overdose. It seemed an odd way to go, seein' as he never did drugs of any kind, not even a smoke. But then, he was a gentle type, and maybe he thought it was the easiest way out.'

'You checked out the truth of that story?' Devereux shot back.

'I did. I had very harsh words with Ballsack and some of his crew, and a few of the other bugger boys that had given the lad a rough time. If they were in any way behind it, I couldn't get it out of them, and I can be persuasive.'

I found it difficult to imagine this small, portly man as the stone cold killer Devereux suggested he was, but experience had taught me that appearances can be very deceptive.

'Your best guess as to what happened?' I asked.

Stills took a cigarette from the breast pocket of his shirt and lit it with an orange plastic lighter.

'I think the loneliness got to him,' he said gently. 'He'd got used to Monty, then me, and suddenly he was in here all by himself again. With solitary, they don't say when you're gettin' out, and for young Timmy that must have seemed even more terrifyin' – I could have been gone forever. I din't have no time to find a babysitter! They just hauled me off. I think the idea of bein' alone and without protection scared the lad to death.'

Devereux looked at me. We both knew it was a perfectly believable hypothesis.

'Thank you, Bob,' Devereux said. 'I'm sorry to have taken up your time.'

''S'alright,' Stills said, drawing on the cigarette. 'Didn't have anythin' else on today.'

I drove back to Garshaigh with a sense of loss that surprised me. It felt as if Tim Fox had become a part of my life, too, and now I was driving with a sad, frightened ghost.

DR B: How does it make you feel when you have to listen to stories like that – when you have to face accounts of terrible abuse and real suffering?

SD: I am trained to set it aside, put it somewhere it can't harm me, and deal with it afterwards.

DR B: And do you do that?

SD: What?

DR B: Deal with it afterwards.

SD: Yes.

DR B: How?

SD: I play music. I go out into the woods or the hills with my dog and walk it off. I cook. I write. It all helps to burn off the bad vibes.

DR B: Is that how you see them? Bad vibes?

SD: It's as good an image as any. I see them as shadows that attach themselves to me, and when I pick up my guitar or get out into the wild places, they all turn into mist and float away.

DR B: All of them?

SD: Most of them, yeah.

DR B: But not all.

SD: Some are harder to shed than others.

DR B: This man, Devereux …

SD: Karl, yes.

DR B: Would you say he is someone you are close to?

SD: I don't know. We're friends. I've never thought about whether we were close or not.

DR B: Think about it now.

SD: I would say we share a mutual sense of respect.

DR B: What do you respect about him?

SD: (*Pauses for several seconds.*) He is certain in everything he does. I have never seen him pause in anything – when he chooses to act he commits totally to whatever course he has set himself. He seems to experience neither fear nor doubt. With Karl there is no self-recrimination – he knows he has done unpalatable things in the past, and he is at peace with that.

DR B: So might it be fairer to say that you *envy* as well as admire him?

SD: (*Said quietly.*) You're probably right, yes.

DR B: Are you at peace with your past, Shane?

SD: I wouldn't be here if I was, would I?

8

A week later school began with a burst of chatter and a clatter of sensible shoes on stone tiles. I found myself immediately busy with some students I'd had the previous year, whom I knew would struggle to adjust to the demands of the more advanced curriculum they would be facing, and several new students, two of whom resented having to attend my classes, which were seen by some as being for the 'special' kids. It was a label I was working hard to shake off, trying to make my sessions as fun and exciting as I could, hoping that some of my charges might actually look forward to coming to class, but it was a reputation I was finding hard to sidestep, an echo from years of tactlessly applied remedial teaching.

At the end of the first day back I sat in my empty classroom, looking at some worksheets I had been doing that afternoon, when there was a knock on the door.

'Come in,' I shouted, too tired from the hectic day to get up and open the door.

A woman I did not know opened the door.

'Is it okay if I have a chat with you for a moment if I'm not disturbing you at your work?' she said, standing hesitantly at the door, seemingly reluctant to come in.

'Not at all. Please come in. How can I help you?'

I motioned at a chair in front of my desk, and she perched on it uncomfortably. She was in her late thirties, pretty but with a tired look, which seemed as though she had been through some stress recently.

'I am Aongus's mother,' she said, referring to one of my new students. 'I just wondered how you found him. Do you think you can help him with his schoolwork, like?'

Some people never get over their distaste for school – it doesn't matter how old they get, or how much they want their own kids to have a good education, they still harbour the emotions of fear, embarrassment and humiliation they had experienced when they were students themselves and some oaf of a teacher had treated them badly. I could see that in this woman's face, too, and badly wanted to put her at ease.

I smiled. 'Yes, I met him this afternoon for the first time. It's early days yet, but I think you should see some solid improvement as the year goes on. He *wants* to learn, which is a huge part of the battle.'

I saw my students either one on one or in groups of no more than three to maximise the impact of the classes, which made it easier for me to get to know them quickly.

'He didn't give you a hard time? He can be fierce rude to some of the teachers.'

'No, we got on fine. Maybe you can help me with something, though.'

A look of terror came over her face, and I immediately regretted my choice of words.

'I just wanted to know what kind of things Aongus likes to do for fun – you know, to relax. Does he like football, or wrestling, or video games or comic books? I try to make these classes as inviting for the kids as I can, and the best way to do this is to use their hobbies and interests, and work those things into the exercises and lessons.'

The woman sighed deeply and shook her head.

'I want him to work hard,' she said after a while. 'He doesn't need easy treatment.'

'I promise I aim to treat Aongus exactly the same as any other student. Does he have any hobbies?'

She shuffled a bit on the seat and finally said, 'He likes that show.'

'A TV programme?'

She nodded.

'Which one?'

'The one with the fightin' and the monsters and that.'

'The *Power Rangers*?'

She nodded, more vigorously this time.

'I don't suppose you know which one of the *Power Rangers* shows he likes best? There's quite a few of them.'

She looked perplexed. 'There's more than one?'

'I'm afraid so. Not to worry. That has been a great help, Mrs Finnegan. Aongus and I can sort out the rest ourselves.'

She remained seated, still looking unhappy.

'Is there anything else you need?'

She cleared her throat and coughed, rooting through an enormous handbag for a tissue.

'They told me you used to work with troubled kids.'

'I did. Still do, sometimes.'

'If I tell you somethin', do you have to tell the social workers about it?'

I put away the papers on my desk and pulled over a refill pad and my pen.

'That depends on what you tell me. If you have information about a child being abused, or you believe a child may be abused in the future, then I have to report that.'

'No, it's nothin' like that.'

'Well, I suppose, outside of those guidelines, it's up to my own discretion then.'

She thought about that, then said rapidly, as if she was afraid she might not go through with it if she didn't get it all out now: 'It's Aongus's brother. Gregory. He keeps runnin' off on me and I don't know what to do.'

I nodded and put the pen back down – the simple matter of a habitual runaway was not something that would require too many detailed reports or a visit to court.

'What age is Gregory?'

'He's eight.'

'Do you know where he goes?'

'Into the woods. He loves them woods, so he does. Always has. Says he's off on an adventure.'

'And does he come back, or do you have to go and fetch him?'

'Both. Trouble is, he often goes there at night, and I don't know he's gone until I go to his room and the bed's empty.'

'That's worrying.'

'I done talked to him about it, but he always just says he's playin'. I locked the doors, but he still gets out. He always seems to be able to find where I've hidden the key, or he gets out through the windows.'

I sat back and thought for a few moments. I had worked with quite a few runners in my time, and the issue usually boiled down to one of two things: the child was either running *from* something or *to* something.

'Is he meeting someone on these expeditions? Another kid maybe? I mean, if he says he's playing …'

'He hasn't mentioned anyone.'

'Is everything okay at home? He hasn't been upset about anything?'

'No.' She bristled at that, but it was a question I had to ask.

'What about at school? Is he being bullied or having a tough time with a teacher?'

'He's a smart one, is Gregory,' she said proudly. 'He's gettin' on great in school.'

'That's good to hear.'

We were quiet for a time. Finally I said, 'Mrs Finnegan, everything kids do is for a reason – Gregory is running away because he's getting something out of doing it. That might be fun or the excitement of escaping; it could be that he's meeting someone he likes or thinks he likes when he's outside; it could be that he's afraid of something you don't know about and he doesn't know how to tell you – he *is* very young. Until we know what's driving him to run, we can't do much about it.'

She listened carefully to this. I could see she was trying very hard to follow what I was saying.

'I'll talk to him,' she said.

'I'm right here if you need any more help,' I said, shaking her hand. 'And stop worrying about Aongus – we're going to get on really well. I promise.'

She bustled out, and I returned to my papers.

I stopped off in the staff room before going home. I had quietly told Maura what I had learned from my visit to Salt Island, and she had listened silently, thanked me, but hadn't spoken to me since. I knew she was grieving, in her way, and I was happy to leave her to it until she came to terms with the difficult truths of Tim's death.

I checked my pigeonhole, where mail and circulars were placed for me to pick up, and there, among the memos and fliers from textbook publishers, was a bright pink envelope, addressed in a flamboyant hand to me at the school. I opened it. Inside was a card, depicting a beaming cartoon man holding out a large bunch of flowers. Above his head were the words *Good Luck!* Inside in the same handwriting as the address was the message: *Wishing you good luck in the coming academic year. Your friend Rex Gifford. So good to get the chance to catch up last week!*

I crumpled it up and dropped it in the bin.

There was another one waiting for me at home, and another in the offices of the newspaper – all identical. I binned them, knowing that sooner or later I was going to have to do something about the person who had sent them.

9

Maura knocked on my door that evening at around eight. I invited her in and opened a bottle of wine.

'I am sorry I bolted today,' she said when we were seated in my living room. Millie was splayed out on the rug between us. 'I tried to prepare myself for what you might find, but I just wasn't ready.'

'There's nothing to apologise for. These are tough things you're trying to deal with. Prison is ugly. People who spend time there end up doing horrible things to one another, and sometimes to themselves. There's no way around that.'

'He didn't deserve it. He was a sweet boy who never hurt anyone in his life. He shouldn't have been in that awful place with those horrendous people. Why couldn't anyone see that?'

'People did. Monty Drew, the man who protected him for most of his sentence, he said as much when I talked to him. I expect the guards realised it too.'

'Why didn't they take better care of him then?'

I thought about that. I hadn't actually talked to any of the prison staff. By taking the route of using Devereux as my eyes and ears I had automatically allied myself with the robbers rather than the cops.

'I don't know,' I admitted. 'The only answer I have is that you can't watch someone twenty-four hours a day, seven days a week. There will always come a moment when your back is turned, even for just a few seconds, and that is just when something bad will happen.'

'I don't think that's a good enough answer,' she said, holding her glass between her hands as if she thought it might warm her. 'I've always held that if we are to call ourselves a truly civilised society, then we must be able to honestly state that each and every person who lives in our communities is valued equally. You see, it's easy for you and me – we're teachers, you're a writer too – we already hold positions because of what we do. We are considered to be educated. No one is going to throw either of us into prison without a very good reason. Poor old Tim, on the other hand, was intellectually disabled; he worked in a job that, regardless of the skill and ability it required, is not particularly . He lived in a poor area and came from a broken home. He had no degrees after his name and no educated friends he could call on to speak up for him. It was easy to cast him aside without a second thought.' She drank some wine. 'Tim, in the last weeks of his life, was reduced to the level of human rubbish. And it makes me sick that I am part of a system that could do that to someone. And I'm not making a dig at you – we are all cogs in the wheel of this great big machine that just grinds up the weak and the vulnerable.'

I blinked, surprised to hear this woman, usually so measured, sounding so bitter and angry.

'That's a pretty grim picture, Maura. Is that really how you see the world?'

She laughed a short, dry chuckle.

'Shane, you've seen a hell of a lot more of the seedy side of life than I have in your former job in child protection,' she said. 'Isn't that how *you* see it?'

'I suppose it is. It just upsets me that you've acquired the same point of view.'

She sighed deeply and sat back on the couch. We were quiet for a long while. I could hear Millie snoring.

'I sort of know one of the guards on The Shaker,' I said at last. 'You're right – I've been treating this as if Tim was the responsibility of the other prisoners, yet in reality, not to mention legally, that just isn't the case. I'll call the prison guard tomorrow, see if he'll meet me and give me his thoughts on what happened.'

'Won't he be less than happy to talk about it, particularly seeing as we're suggesting that the accepted verdict is incorrect?'

'He'll get over it,' I said.

'You would have liked Tim,' Maura said. 'And I think he would have liked you.'

'Almost everyone does,' I said deadpan.

10

The prison guard in question, a short but steely Dundalk man named Bernie, was not due on shift until the following evening, so I left a message asking him to ring me.

Despite the fact that it was only my second day back, I found that I was already comfortably ensconced in the rhythm of teaching. I relished the give-and-take of education, and found that no matter how allegedly 'disabled' a student was, I rarely finished a class without having learned something myself. Most of the kids I worked with didn't exactly enjoy their time in school, but I did my best to make the hours they spent there as much fun as possible.

This did not always go smoothly. That Tuesday Aongus Finnegan stomped into my empty classroom, clearly in a very bad mood. He flung his bag on the floor beside his desk and sat down in his chair, his arms folded in an almighty huff.

I pretended not to notice, sorting through some papers and not looking up. I purposely made him wait, hoping that whatever was bothering him would sort itself out in his head. Truthfully, I knew there was little chance of this happening, but I try to see the glass as half-full.

Finally I went and sat down opposite the sulking boy.

'What's up, Aongus?'

'Nuthin'.'

'That's not true. I can see you're annoyed about something. Now, you can continue sitting there looking like someone has nicked your favourite tee-shirt, or we can talk about it and get some work done.'

'I don't care if we gets no work done. I don't wanna be in no retard class anyways.'

'Is that what you think this is?'

'In my last school they told my ma I was a slow learner. That means they thinks I'm retarded.'

'It doesn't,' I said. 'It means you have difficulties with some of the stuff you have to learn, but a lot of that comes down to the way it's taught. I'm not saying I'm going to do any better than your last teacher, but I *am* prepared to try some different ways of looking at how you approach reading and writing.'

'Don't wanna learn how to fuckin' read!' he snapped.

I didn't budge – just sat watching him. I've dealt with enough angry kids in my time not to be perturbed by a temper tantrum.

'You'd prefer not to learn?'

He looked at me through slitted eyes.

'Yeah, I would.'

'Okay then.'

He sat up, clearly puzzled by my reaction.

'Okay? But you gots to teach me.'

I grinned.

'How old are you, Aongus?'

'Thirteen.'

'Right. Now, by the age of thirteen you are still struggling with literacy. I am, certainly, paid to try and help you with that, but if I were to fail, do you think I'd get fired, or told off or even asked any questions about it?'

He looked unhappy at that.

'I'll answer the question for you,' I said. 'No, I wouldn't. No one, except possibly your mother, would really care at all. And d'you know what that means?'

He shook his head.

'It means that I will get paid no matter what we do in here. Want to play video games? Want to watch a movie? Want to just sit and shoot the shit? We can do that. No odds to me one way or the other.'

He looked as if he might burst into tears now. His lower lip had developed a marked tremble.

'You don't mean that. You has to teach me. I'll tell. I'll go talk to Mr Taylor and you'll get the sack.'

'There's the door. You know where his office is.'

I sat back, put my feet up on the desk and produced a magazine from the open drawer at my elbow. I had bought it on the way home the previous evening – it was a brightly coloured publication entitled *Power Rangers Megaforce* and had a large picture of the colourfully clad superheroes on the front cover, one of whom was holding what looked like a hi-tech crossbow.

Aongus went to stand up but, seeing what I was reading, stopped dead in his tracks.

'What's that?' he asked.

'This?' I said, peering at him over the top of the magazine. 'Oh, it's just something I'm reading. One of the other students told me all about this show, and I really got into it. When I like something, I try to learn as much as I can about it. So I bought this. It's pretty good.'

'I … I really like *Megaforce*,' he said haltingly. 'I loves *Power Rangers Ninja Storm* too. That's the best one.'

I put down the magazine.

'Yeah? I've never seen that one.'

In a voice trembling with excitement, the boy began to tell me how his favourite television programme was all about a bunch of students in a school for Ninjas. These kids were the worst students in the school (all slow learners), but when an evil Ninja master attacked, intent on imprisoning every martial artist in the land, our heroes somehow survived, and, with their teacher, formed a team dedicated to stopping him and saving their classmates. I could immediately see how the storyline would appeal to this young teenager – so angry, yet so in need of validation and approval. It was the classic outsider fantasy: the derided and neglected prove their worth and are hailed as heroes by their peers. I leafed through the magazine with Aongus, reading bits and pieces from it aloud, discussing the many photos, allowing him to explain the subtleties of various characters and plot points. The rest of the class passed quickly, and before we both knew it, the bell was ringing to let us know that it was time for the mid-morning break. As he was going I tossed the magazine over to him.

'Why don't you take it home? I'm finished reading it.'

He grinned, clearly delighted.

'You sure?'

'Positive. Why don't you have a go at reading some of the comic strips in it. Comics are really easy to read, because the pictures help you to work out what the story is, and what the people might be saying. Tomorrow you can show me how well you did.'

'Is it okay if I gets me brother to help me? He loves *Power Rangers* too.'

'Gregory?'

'Yeah. He's a real good reader, he is. Much betterer than me.'

I smiled.

'Of course. Sometimes sharing a book with someone makes it even more fun. Are you and Gregory close?'

'Yeah. We lives out in the country, so there isn't a lot of other kids around. It's just me and Greggy mostly. Well, he says he has anudder friend, but I'm not so sure.'

I perked up at this.

'He says he has another friend? Surely you've met them.'

'No. He says there's this little boy calls to him at night. He sneaks off into the woods to play with him when we's all asleep. I asked him to wake me, so I could go and play too, but he never does. I think he's makin' it up.'

This was strange indeed. Was there another runaway in the area, a child who had somehow sought out Gregory?

'Did he tell you this boy's name?'

'Yeah. He says his name is Thomas. Listen, I gotta go. Thanks for the comic book.'

I decided that perhaps Mrs Finnegan's fears for her son might have some foundation. Who was this Thomas, and why was he looking for playmates in the hours of darkness?

11

Tweedy's was one of the larger pubs in Garshaigh, and on Thursday nights it hosted a music session that attracted folkies from miles around. I was a fairly regular attender of these gatherings: the pub had a nice, olde worlde feel, with an open fire on winter nights and cool shade during the summer months, and the beer was always of exceptional quality. The punters who came to listen managed to balance boisterousness with respect for the tunes and songs, so in general a good night was had by all.

That first Thursday of term I decided to pay Tweedy's a visit as a kind of send-off to the long, lazy summer I had had, so I packed up my guitar and harmonicas and made the short stroll through the balmy evening to add my voice to the ragtag choir.

There were probably twenty other musicians gathered about the room that evening: fiddle, accordion and concertina players, a percussionist with bones and a bodhrán, several guitarists, a bouzouki player, and a couple of ukulele strummers to round out the mix. The system in Tweedy's was simple – Mike Jones, a long-haired fifty-something-year-old, who played a beautiful old American Gibson guitar, always opened with a song (that night he treated us to Dylan's 'Just Like a Woman'), and then it was the turn of whoever was on his immediate right, and so on around the assembled musicians. Everyone was expected to take a turn – either to sing or to play a tune, and anyone who wished to could join in. Sometimes people from the audience shouted a request, which an individual was at liberty to play or not: this was an utterly democratic set-up, and everyone seemed content with the arrangement.

I had a couple of pints of Guinness and enjoyed myself tremendously. Sometimes, if a tune or song I liked was being played I added a lick or some harmony, but just as often I sipped my drink and let the music wash over me. There was plenty of chat between numbers, questions about where a particular piece of music had been learned, comments on a bit of work someone had done on their instrument (Joe, the bouzouki player, had brought along a hundred-year-old mandolin he had just renovated, and that was the source of much comment and questioning). My turn came around and I sang the old Grateful Dead number 'Friend of the Devil' – I've always liked the imagery in it: the harassed protagonist, fleeing prison, borrows money from the Devil to make it back home, only to discover that in his absence a woman he was having an affair with behind his wife's back has announced that she is pregnant with his child. His parting line as he heads for the hills ('the woman says she's got my child, but he don't look like me!') always garnered a laugh, and the rollicking, thumping rhythm never failed to get the group really cooking.

I had just finished a harmonica solo and brought the song to a close when I sensed someone come up behind me. I had a harmonica harness around my neck (so I could play the harmonica while also picking the guitar), which made turning difficult, but before I could move the person said, right into my ear:

'I'd heard you could play, and just had to check that out.'

A hand was placed on my neck and, before I had time to move, a searing pain shot down my right side as a nerve cluster was deftly pinched, paralysing me for a second. The pain was so intense, I couldn't even cry out. Through the agony I recognised the voice, and as soon as I was released, I twisted in my chair. Rex Gifford, smiling as if we were the best of friends, stepped back quickly, putting several feet between us. We stared at each other for a few moments – my chair was wedged between two others, so I could not get to him without tossing my guitar aside and then standing up on my seat and jumping over the back, an action I thought would take far too long to make it effective.

'Did you get my cards?' Gifford asked.

Now I did stand. Eoin, the uke player beside me, seemed to notice something was wrong, and got up too.

'Everything alright there, Shane?' he asked.

'No,' I said through clenched teeth.

Eoin looked at Gifford. 'Who's this?'

Rex smiled and, blowing me a kiss, ducked out a door to his left and was gone.

By the time I got to the carpark there was no sign of him. My arm was still numb, and I found I could not play for the rest of the night. I also decided that a visit to the police station was on the cards for the following day.

12

I sat in an interview room in the Garshaigh police station the following morning, and showed Garda Harry Doyle the dark bruise that had formed on my shoulder. He was a young officer, possibly in his mid-twenties, slimly built with a blond crew cut. He and I had a working relationship from my covering the courts for the newspaper.

'You have witnesses?' he asked.

The room was empty save for a desk and two chairs. The cream paint on the walls was cracked and peeling. It was not a pleasant space, but then the reason I was there was not pleasant either.

I sighed. 'No. I was with a large group who can attest to the fact that Gifford was there, but the limits that have been placed on his behaviour do not prevent him from going to pubs or hanging around me. No one saw him touch me.'

Doyle closed his notebook as I put my tee-shirt back on.

'Shane, you know how this works as well as I do.'

'Yeah.'

'You can press charges, but it probably won't go anywhere.'

'Rex Gifford has a record of violent crime,' I shot back.

'Against teenage girls, which, respectfully, you aren't.'

I suddenly felt very angry.

'He's not stupid, Harry. He's playing me and he knows just how to make it hurt – I mean, what am I supposed to do? Ignore him until he does something really serious?'

'Of course not,' Doyle said, his voice softening as he realised how agitated I was. 'Do you want me to have a word with him?'

'I would love you to,' I said, rubbing my eyes; I had not slept and was tired and irritable. 'Except he'll know you can't back up the warning with anything. Even if I did run into him again after your chat, what could I do about it?'

'If you were able to establish a pattern to his harassment and a reasonable cause for fear, you could get a restraining order.'

'And again, he'd have had to have done something serious for that to stick.'

'Not necessarily. With the history you and he have, being able to demonstrate that he is making a nuisance of himself would probably work.'

'And how would I prove the nuisance factor?'

'The cards he sent you?'

'None of which say anything threatening or even rude, and all of which I threw in the bin.'

Doyle was quiet for a moment.

'I'm sorry,' he said finally. 'Keep me informed, okay? If he puts one more foot out of line I'll haul him in.'

'Thank you,' I said, without really feeling any sense of relief.

Gifford had outmanoeuvred me. Again.

DR B: Outmanoeuvred you?

SD: Yes.

DR B: Did you feel you were in a kind of competition with this man?

SD: No, of course I didn't.

DR B: Yet the language you use – it's as if you and he are squaring off against each other. It's quite a macho thing to do.

SD: You're reading too much into it.

DR B: Am I? You're in a profession that a lot of people might see as feminine – you work with kids. I don't think it hard to understand you would be attracted to alpha males. Your friend Devereux is a classic example – he is a violent man a lot of people fear, yet you gravitate towards him. You go out of your way to take on a job that brings you to prisons and into conversations with criminals. And Rex Gifford, whom you would seem to classify as a kind of nemesis figure for you, fits that criteria, too. He is a worthy adversary, isn't he? He's brilliant and resourceful and about as bad as can be.

SD: You're painting it as if I wanted to have this guy on my case.

DR B: I'm not saying that. What I'm trying to get you to think about is that there are aspects to this person's character you admire – his intellect, his survival skills, his tenacity.

SD: Doctor, if there was ever someone I could say that I hated without reservation, it would be Rex Gifford.

DR B: Have you ever worked with anyone in the past whom you both loved and hated at the same time?

SD: Well there would have been people who had done bad things, but in whom I could see good points …

DR B: And does Rex Gifford not have good points?

SD: He performs well. He can be charming and witty and seem like the nicest person in the world, but he is as evil a man as any I have met.

DR B: Is there really such a thing as an evil person, Shane?

SD: I believe there is, yes.

13

The Finnegans lived on a narrow by-road that wound through the woods and hills surrounding Garshaigh, about six kilometres north of the town. Mrs Finnegan, whose name I eventually learned was Orla, had given me directions that seemed to involve taking a road off a road off another road, none of which had any names or identifying features, and I got hopelessly lost. There was no mobile phone coverage either, since the hills and rocky crags that rose on either side of the laneway served to dampen reception completely. Finally, almost an hour after I'd set out, and by accident more than design, I pulled up outside the little house, a simple two-up/two-down with ivy clinging to the front wall, and parked against the ditch as tightly as I could.

Orla met me at the door wearing a rumpled tracksuit, her hair looking uncombed.

'Thank you for coming,' she said. 'You found us okay, anyway.'

I smiled and let that one go.

She showed me into the kitchen, which was just about big enough to hold a small dining table. Gregory was there, reading the *Power Rangers* magazine I had given to Aongus. He looked like his older brother but in miniature, with darker hair and a slightly quizzical expression. I sat opposite him and explained who I was, and that his mother had asked me to come out to visit so we could talk about his night-time activities; I didn't think there was anything to be gained by pretending I was there to hang out and play some games – Gregory was clever enough to see through that. The lad listened as I spoke, but said nothing.

'So, d'you want to chat about this kid Thomas?'

Gregory shook his head.

'Why not?'

A shrug.

'Your mum isn't mad at you, Gregory. She's just worried. All we're trying to do is keep you safe. You understand that, don't you? Going out into the woods at night could be really dangerous.'

That elicited no response at all – the boy just stared at me with his huge brown eyes.

'Here's a thing I sometimes do with kids who find talking about stuff difficult,' I said. 'I'll tell you what I think's going on, and you can shake your head if I'm wrong, or nod if I'm right. That way, you're telling me but you don't have to talk unless you want to. How does that sound?'

There was the barest semblance of a nod, so I ploughed on.

'Your name is Gregory Finnegan.'

A nod.

'You have pink hair and three ears.'

A vigorous shake of the head.

'No?'

Shake, combined with just the touch of a smile.

'You go to school in Garshaigh.'

Nod.

'Your teacher is a giant bunny rabbit called Malcolm.'

A laugh now, and a shake.

'You have a brother called Aongus.'

Nod.

'You like the *Power Rangers*.'

Strong nod.

'You like playing games on the Xbox.'

Shake.

'The PlayStation 3?'

Nod.

'You like football?'

Nod.

'You have a friend called Thomas.'

Nod. Yes.

'And you know him from school.'

Shake. No.

'He lives near you. Like a neighbour.'

Yes.

'You met him at a football match.'

No.

'At church.'

No.

'At the beach.'

No.

'When you were shopping in Garshaigh with your mother.'

No.

Grasping at straws: 'You met him on the internet?'

Gregory laughed and shook his head.

I sat back, flat out of ideas.

'How'd you meet him, Gregory?'

The little boy fiddled with the sleeve of his jumper for a moment. Then, almost in a whisper:

'I heared him.'

'You *heared* him? What do you mean?'

'I heared him crying.'

It was my turn to shake my head, this time.

'I still don't get it, Gregory,' I said. 'You'll have to explain it to me better.'

Hopping down from his chair, the boy took my hand.

'Come on. I'll show you.'

Gregory's bedroom was tiny, too. It had wallpaper Father Ted's house would be proud to own, over which posters of Formula One cars, Power Rangers and Manchester United players had been stuck. A small window overlooked the woods.

'He was down there,' Gregory said, opening the latch on the window and swinging it wide.

'In your back garden?'

'No. Just there. Beyond the fence.'

The Finnegans' garden had been cordoned off with a slightly rusted iron fence, which someone had painted red several years ago. Beyond it was line upon line of trees.

'So he was in the woods, then?'

Gregory nodded.

'He was cryin'. He waked me up.'

'Right. You had just gone to bed, and you were reading a book or whatever, and he called for you to come out and play?'

'No, you ain't listenin'. It was real late. I'd been in bed a long time. I woked up cause I heared someone cryin' like they was real sad or somethin'. I thought it was my mam, but then I listened and it wasn't. I knew it was a kid. And the more I listened, I knew it wasn't Aongus. And then I listened more, and I heared it was comin' from outside, so I got out of my bed and pulled back the curtain, and I looked out.'

I sat down on the edge of the bed, fascinated by what I was hearing.

'It was real dark, so I had to look hard, but then I seen him.'

'This kid Thomas?'

Gregory nodded.

'I din't know that was his name then. I just saw a little kid. He was standing right under that tree, the big one nearest our fence. I opened the window and looked out and I saw he was small – I'm the second shortest kid in my class, and Thomas is *a lot* smaller than me. He was wearin' real old clothes – he always wears the same things, I don' think he has any others – and he has black hair and white, white skin. When he saw me he stopped cryin' and looked up at me, and he kind of made a move with his hand, like he was askin' me to go down and talk to him.'

'And you did.'

'He looked real sad and lonely.'

'That was very kind of you, Gregory, but it sounds to me as if Thomas is maybe in some kind of trouble. Where does he live? I think I should have a chat with his mum and dad.'

'He don't got no mam and dad,' Gregory said.

'Does he live with his grandparents?'

Shake. No.

'His aunt and uncle?'

No.

'Foster family?'

No.

'Okay. Tell me.'

'He lives on his own in the woods. He don't got no family, and he don't go to school. It's only him, and he told me he just wants someone to play with him. We're bestest friends, him 'n' me.'

'It sounds like classic imaginary friend material,' I told Orla Finnegan over a cup of tea a short time later. 'It's a typical fantasy for a kid who is isolated and longs for a friend.'

'What can I do?'

'Well, keep locking the doors and perhaps put a bolt on them higher than he can reach. Maybe get one of those baby monitors so you can hear if he tries to wander, and think about getting him involved in some clubs or having some of his school friends come over from time to time. Thomas is serving a purpose just now. If you take that purpose away, you'll find he goes with it. Children can be very tough on imaginary friends – in my experience they get dropped without ceremony.'

I left that afternoon convinced of what I had just told Gregory's mother. I was wrong, but it was a fortnight before I found that out.

14

I met my friend Bernie, who worked as a guard on The Shaker, at six in the morning the following Saturday. He had just come off shift and we went for breakfast at a café on the docks, a cluttered room with five tables covered in check tablecloths and a short menu written in yellow chalk on a blackboard hung over the counter.

Bernie was a small man, all muscle and attitude, his greying dark hair shaved close to his head, a scar from an old brawl running in a ragged line down his cheek. We had met ten years before, when I had been attacked while visiting the incarcerated parent of some kids I was working with. Bernie had managed to drag me away from the fray while my assailant, a giant with the mental age of a toddler, was subdued. I was struck by the little guard's funereal sense of humour in such stark grimness, and we stayed in touch.

As we ordered food and sipped coffee the early-morning crowd drifted in.

'I have never got used to the night shift,' he said. 'Always makes me feel like I'm jetlagged.'

'I didn't mind it. It can be quieter than working days.'

'I prefer to be kept busy. It's good to see you, mate, but why are you here?'

I told him about Tim Fox.

'Tim,' Bernie said. 'Shit, he was a sad case. Yeah, I remember him well.'

'And?'

'What do you want to know?'

'What've you got?'

Bernie took a deep breath.

'He was a good kid who probably shouldn't have been locked up. But you know, I don't sentence them, and I don't ask questions. My job is to keep things running smoothly inside those walls, and that's what I concern myself with.'

Our food arrived – a full Irish for Bernie, an omelette for me.

'All I'm looking for are your impressions,' I said. 'I think I've been coming at it from the wrong end.'

'How so?'

'I've been asking other prisoners. I'd like your take on what happened to Tim – as you've already said, his welfare was your job.'

'And a damn fine mess I made of it.'

'That's not what I mean, and you know it.'

'Tim Fox is a classic case of the system derailing. It's not a new story. He came in pretty green and scared out of his wits, and the place chewed him up. And the drugs finished him.'

I looked up from my food sharply.

'I was told he never touched dope.'

'Well, you were told wrong. He wasn't someone who used stuff every day, but he surely dipped into it from time to time.'

'How come you know this and his cellmates didn't?'

'Maybe because lying to you doesn't get me anywhere.'

'Why would Monty Drew and Bob Stills lie?'

Bernie motioned with his mug for a refill and sat back.

'Perhaps saying they lied is too harsh.'

'They both said he never so much as smoked a cigarette. They were amazed that he took an overdose.'

'The kid is dead, right?'

'Yes.'

'So what is to be gained by trashing his memory? If you and your friend want to continue believing he was as pure as the driven snow, what harm is there in it? In a way, they were being kind.'

'I want the truth, Bernie. A rose-tinted version of it doesn't help me.'

'Monty and Bob were invested in the idea that they had protected the lad. Part of that involves maintaining his innocence. Almost everyone on that rock will tell you they didn't do whatever it was got them locked up. They very jealously guard that image of who they wish they were. To suggest that Tim was becoming tainted by prison would compromise who he wanted to be and who his associates wanted him to be, and even after his death none of the boys would want to do that.'

'So what you're saying is that I've got sucked into jailhouse psychology.'

'Welcome to my world.'

We ate in silence for a while.

'It's not so bizarre that he took an overdose then?' I said finally. 'He was, at the very least, an occasional user?'

'That's about it, yeah. But there's one more thing.'

'What?'

'I don't think he topped himself.'

'What?'

'Well, not on purpose anyway. I heard that Tim used stuff when things got tough for him. When he was getting beat up and raped, he was off his head a lot of the time – it was how he coped with it. In those last days, when Stills got sent down and Tim was on his own, I'd say he was using again, 'cause he was terrified out of his wits. But there was a bad consignment of drugs that had been smuggled in that week. It'd been cut with some poison or other; I don't know what shit they use to pad the stuff out, but it was lethal. I've never asked, and I never looked at the medical reports on him, but if I had to guess, I'd say he got hold of some of that and shot up, thinking it was his usual fix. He would have been dead before he knew what hit him.'

'A stupid accident.'

'Yep.'

'I don't even know how to process this information.'

'What's to process? It doesn't change anything. Tim Fox still shouldn't have been in there. Never should have had access to narcotics. A kid with an intellectual disability should have been better cared for. It's as much a tragedy right now as it was fifteen minutes ago.'

'I know. It's just that Maura, my colleague, will be even more heartbroken when she hears the new version of events.'

'So don't tell her. Let her believe whatever helps her sleep more easily.'

'Maybe I will.'

'You should,' Bernie said, pushing his plate aside. 'The Shaker stains everyone and everything that comes into contact with it. It always has. Don't let it spread its filth farther than it needs to. Leave her with her good memories.'

All the way back to Garshaigh I pondered what Bernie had said, but I was still none the wiser when I got home. Millie didn't have any ideas either, so we went for a walk on the beach and let the wind and the spray blow away some of the unhappy feelings I was experiencing.

15

I left school the following Monday at five, and Rex Gifford was across the road, hands in his pockets, leaning against the wall, staring right at me. I paused, on the verge of storming over and challenging him. He smiled and waved, my ominous expression clearly not bothering him much. Clenching my teeth, I turned on my heel and stalked home. As far as I could see, he didn't follow me.

When I walked to work at the newspaper offices the next day, I saw him sitting at a table outside the café where I usually bought my morning coffee. I decided to forego the Americano and stomped on past. He wasn't there (or I didn't see him at least) when I went to get lunch, nor was he evident at the end of the school day, but that Saturday when I went to the farmers' market to buy some groceries, I spotted him through the crowd several times, though he was never there when I looked again. I thought that I was probably getting paranoid.

Every night before bed, Millie and I went for a walk. We did a circuit of the main thoroughfare – it took only about fifteen minutes and gave Millie a chance to deal with her ablutions before I locked her in for the night, while I enjoyed the peace of the late-night town. It gave me a chance to be alone with my thoughts in the cool night air.

I left Millie off the lead during these late meanders. There was no traffic and I had never met another dog walker, so I saw no reason not to give her free roam. Every now and again she would take off after a cat, but even that did not happen often, so we usually strolled along at a leisurely pace, me doing a little window shopping and listening to the wind, Millie snuffling here and there.

On this particular Wednesday night, our walk began as usual. We reached the top of the town and turned to begin our walk homeward. At that point there is a narrow alleyway that runs between two shops, and Millie, who was just ahead of me, stopped suddenly at the mouth of it, her ears erect, her tail straight out, on point. Thinking back, I am almost certain I heard a low whistle, but I cannot be sure. At any rate, in a burst of movement Millie bolted up the alley helter-skelter. I thought nothing of it – a cat or a feral fox had attracted her attention, I reasoned, and she'd be back when she got bored of the sport.

I had gone maybe fifteen yards up the street when I realised she was not following me. I paused and looked back. The mouth of the alleyway was simply a rectangle of dim shadow in the street lights. I whistled sharply, which was the signal I used to call her to me urgently – she usually responded immediately, but in truth, Millie is a wilful dog and has never been beyond ignoring me if something more interesting has her attention.

I retraced my steps and called her name. Still no response.

Cursing her now, I made my way up the alley, and there, at the end, was my greyhound, hungrily munching on something. She looked at me sheepishly, as if she knew she was doing something I would not approve of.

'What have you got there?' I asked, shooing her aside (she moved about an inch, snaffling another mouthful before I could grab her collar).

Kneeling, I saw it was a mound of what looked to be ground beef. There were bins all about, so I reasoned that someone had thrown the stuff away, and an animal had pulled it out of whichever receptacle it had been deposited in and had been eating it when Millie happened along. I couldn't see a bag, which I was sure it must have been in, but that could have blown away.

'Come on, greedy guts,' I said, and led my still masticating friend back to the street. 'You know, it'd be nice if you occasionally did what I asked.'

Millie continued to ignore me, so I gave up.

I was awakened from sleep a couple of hours later by my dog whining, a high-pitched cry that soon became a plaintive wail. Alarmed, I got up and went to the kitchen, where she always slept. Millie was lying on her side, a pool of frothy vomit on the floor beside her, clearly in a great deal of pain.

'You've done it this time,' I said, ruefully checking the puke. 'What've I told you about eating things you find on the street?'

There was very little of the meat in Millie's vomit. Still curled into a foetal position, the dog whined again. My heart went out to her, but I knew I had to act fast.

'You're not going to like this,' I said, and mixed up a glass of salt and mustard powder with some water, and holding her head back, poured it down Millie's throat. Moaning miserably, she scuttled into the corner and threw up the contents of her stomach. The meat was clearly visible now. Relieved, I picked her up and brought her into the living room, putting her on the couch. She seemed more comfortable now and lay against me shivering, but seemingly no longer hurting. I stroked her black flanks while speaking gently to her, telling her she was going to be alright. I felt as if I had been through the wringer myself, but I didn't want to take any chances so, despite the fact that it was very late, I rang my vet, Clancy, who answered sleepily. I explained the situation and he told me to bring Millie into the surgery, which he lived above, right away.

I scooped a little of the regurgitated meat into a plastic bag and cleaned up the rest.

On examination, Millie seemed to be over the worst of it, but my still sleepy veterinarian said he had better keep her in for observation.

'This is what she ate,' I said, passing him the bag with its semi-digested contents.

'You're sure she didn't eat anything else? Some poisons are slow-acting.'

'I'm certain.'

'Okay, I'll have a look at it. Call me tomorrow and we'll see how she's doing.'

Begrudgingly, I hugged Millie and went home.

I rang Clancy at ten the next morning.

'She's doing fine. Ate a hearty breakfast and seems none the worse for wear.'

'I'll be right over. Any thoughts on what she ingested?'

'Obviously I don't have a full lab facility here, and I'll have to send away the sample you gave me to have it thoroughly checked, but I think it was pesticide. This is a rural area, so there's loads of it about.'

'How did it get into a pile of meat?'

'People hereabouts use it as a poison, to kill rats mostly. I think your Millie might just have been in the wrong place at the wrong time.'

'Story of her life,' I said, laughing. 'I'll be there in ten minutes.'

'I'll tell her to pack her things.'

Millie seemed moderately pleased to see me, and to celebrate her good health I took her for a run in the woods. I thought that she was still a bit reserved, but by the time we headed for home her usual loping gait had almost returned.

We got back to town around lunchtime. I planned on having a quick sandwich and then heading into the newspaper office to catch up on some paperwork – I was behind with my journalistic duties, having taken the morning off, but I thought that by working a little later than usual, I could make up for lost ground. I dumped my coat on the couch in the living room and stopped dead.

There, sitting in the middle of the coffee table, was a note written in thick, neat block capitals on plain white paper. It read: GLAD MILLIE IS FEELING BETTER. I turned the paper over – there was no signature and no name – in fact, there were no identifying features at all. I checked every window and every door, but there was no sign of a break in, and nothing was missing. Other than the note, everything was just as I had left it. If the message had not been there, I would have never known anyone had been in my house.

But someone had. Rex Gifford had been in my home, and it looked like he had tried to kill my dog.

Now I was really angry.

16

I'd like to say I was able to put thoughts of Gifford from my head that afternoon, but that would be a lie. So unnerved was I by the break-in that I could not leave Millie in the house alone – he had already hurt her once – so I took her to work with me. Robert Chaplin, my boss, was out of the office (thankfully), so she curled up at my feet and slept there for the afternoon while I got on with the business of writing the three articles I had promised to finish by teatime.

It was not any easy task. I found my mind wandering, my thoughts turning time and again to where Rex Gifford might be and what havoc he might be wreaking. I toyed with the idea of bringing the note he had left to the police, but I knew that would be pointless – the text could have been written by anyone, and I would have bet all my possessions that the writing paper could be bought in any stationery shop in the country and that there would be no fingerprints on it other than my own. The afternoon dragged on into evening, and as the hands of the clock crawled past eight, I completed my last piece, a terse little discussion on local government spending, printed off a hard copy and left the bundle on Chaplin's desk.

The light had started to go out of the evening when Millie and I got down to the street, but it was a pleasant, warm dusk. I paused to lock up, and turned to see Rex Gifford crossing the road, his hand outstretched, a smile across his face.

'Shane old boy, fancy meeting you here,' he said.

I saw red. All sense left me and I found myself bubbling over with a rage I could not suppress. As soon as he was within reach, I grabbed him by his lapels and lifted him off his feet, slamming him into the wall as hard as I could.

'I see she's made a full recovery,' Gifford said, forcing out the words because most of the breath had been knocked out of him. 'You got my message, I take it?'

I pulled back my fist. I was going to blot out that laughing, maniacal face.

I was ready to deliver the blow when some level of reason returned. A look of utter glee was emblazoned across Gifford's features. His breathing was laboured but, other than that, he was unharmed. I realised his eyes were darting back and forth over my shoulder – and then I heard voices and knew there were people passing by across the road. Witnesses.

I had played right into his hands. If I hit him, he would press charges. Any moves he had made against me were so subtle, so carefully administered that I had no way of proving they had happened, but here I was, manhandling him on Garshaigh's main thoroughfare in full view of anyone who happened to be about.

I dropped him, the look of triumph immediately leaving his visage.

'I … I bet your mutt cried like a little bitch,' he said, not ready to give up yet. 'I'd say she shat blood.'

I whistled and Millie trotted after me. I didn't look back, which is probably just as well, because I was crying with temper. And maybe just a little shame.

DR B: Why didn't you hit him?

SD: It's what he wanted me to do.

DR B: He nearly killed your dog.

SD: If he wanted to kill her, she wouldn't be lying across my kitchen floor right now. No, he wanted to scare me, and hurt her, but I don't think he wanted to kill her.

DR B: You were really angry though. I could even hear it in your voice as you talked about it. He got to you.

SD: Yes.

DR B: Do you often feel like resorting to violence?

SD: No. I would say that I rarely feel the need to lash out.

DR B: That would indicate that there have been times when you have lashed out.

SD: Yes. There have been one or two, but when that happens, it means I have lost control and that is not something I relish.

DR B: Control is very important to you, isn't it?

SD: Yes.

DR B: Why do you think that is?

SD: You're the shrink. You tell me.

DR B: I don't know. It seems to me that you spend a huge amount of time rushing about, trying to get the world under some level of control – it's as if you're trying to shape it into something manageable.

SD: And is that such a bad thing?

DR B: I could say you are setting yourself up for failure – the world is what it is and no amount of struggling is going to change that. It could make you very fatalistic.

SD: I am not a fatalist, Doctor. I'm an idealist.

DR B: I think there is a very fine line between those two things, Shane.

17

I got a call a week later during my lunch break. I was sitting in my empty classroom marking some papers, and saw it was the number of the local garda station.

'Shane, Harry Doyle here.'

'Yes, hello.'

'Shane, I believe you've had some dealings with a youngster called Gregory Finnegan.'

'Uh, yes, I have. Is there a problem with Gregory?'

'Could you drop by the station this evening, Shane? I'm on until eight. I'd just like your thoughts on an issue that has come up. It's nothing to worry about, I'm sure – Mrs Finnegan told me you'd been consulted by the family about Gregory's disappearances.'

'Has he been going out at night again?'

'He has. Could you call in and see me?'

'I finish here at four. I'll be right over then.'

Harry was waiting for me at the front desk when I arrived, and brought me through to the interview room where we had last talked.

'We received a call from Orla Finnegan two nights ago,' he began, reading from notes he had made on a small pad. 'She said that she had looked in on her son Gregory at about twelve thirty that night, and found his bed empty. She made a search of the house but he wasn't anywhere. She awoke her other son, Aongus, and they reconnoitred the area about their abode, an action which did not serve to locate Gregory. At this point she called the station. I went out to the house, accompanied by Garda Casey Warren. We ventured as far as we could into the woods, in search of the boy, but it proved fruitless, not to mention dangerous, and we were forced to abandon the attempt after an hour. I remained with the family throughout the night, but Gregory did not return, and at first light, with two other officers, we made another search of the area.'

Doyle took a photograph from an envelope on the table and passed it to me.

'I observed a set of footprints leading from the fence to the area below Gregory's bedroom window.'

The photo showed a close-up of one of these prints, with a measuring tape laid beside it to show the scale. There was a kind of zigzag pattern within the indentation of the foot, which made me think of a trainer or tennis shoe, but it didn't mean much to me.

'I take it I'm looking at a child's footprint?'

'A child or a very small adult, yes.'

'Fuck,' I said. 'Thomas is real.'

'It would seem that another person is involved,' Harry Doyle agreed. 'I also noted a set of tracks, which we were subsequently able to confirm were Gregory's, leading from the back door, apparently meeting with the owner of the unknown set, and leading through the fence and into the trees. Using these I was – though not easily – able to follow Gregory and eventually track him down.'

'I advised her to put a bolt on the back door.'

'It would appear she did not follow your advice.'

'You found the boy?'

'Approximately five miles from his home, in an area of dense woodland perhaps a quarter of a mile from the beach at Kiltoley.'

'Thank God. And this other kid, Thomas?'

'When we found Gregory Finnegan, he was alone. He did indicate that another child, a boy he referred to as Thomas, was nearby – he said they were playing hide-and-go-seek, but I called and looked very thoroughly, and could find no one, although it seems clear he did leave his home in the company of another person.'

'The tracks?'

'The ground had become very boggy and wet there – it was barely possible to discern any markings at all, let alone tell sets apart. We were lucky to find him.'

I shook my head.

'I can't believe it,' I said. 'I was certain Thomas was just a figment of Gregory's imagination.'

'It appears that he is, indeed, a real person. Shane, we're chasing our tail on this one. It looks like Gregory is very much at risk, and this child Thomas seems to be in real danger too. At the very least, he is being seriously neglected. Did Gregory tell you anything when you interviewed him that might help us to locate this child's family?'

'Gregory told me Thomas lives on his own in the woods,' I said. 'It's what made me think it was just a story. According to young Greg, Thomas is a Peter Pan type of character, living wild and free.'

'I've gone over our files and there are no reports of runaway children. He must be living with a family somewhere.'

'I'd check in with social services if I were you. They might have some sense of who he is.'

'I rang them this morning,' Doyle said, closing his notebook and putting away the photograph. 'They didn't know of any children who fit the description. They're keeping an eye out, but I'm not hopeful.'

'I'll have a think and if anything occurs to me, I'll let you know.'

'I'd appreciate it,' Doyle said, and showed me out.

I thought about what he'd told me for the rest of the night – the image of two tiny figures, hand in hand, being swallowed up by the trees, impossible to get out of my head.

18

That evening I met Maura for a drink in Stanbridge's, which was the bar most of the teachers in Garshaigh frequented. It was low-ceilinged and dark, a real turf fire smouldering at the back of the room and The Beatles' *White Album* playing quietly over the stereo system.

Maura was there when I arrived, a barely touched Bacardi and Coke sitting on a beer mat in front of her. After I'd bought a glass of Bushmills, I recounted what Bernie had told me about Tim Fox in terms as gentle as I could formulate. She took it better than I had expected, although she was clearly shaken.

'You did your best, Shane, and I'm grateful for it.'

'So did you.'

'Perhaps. It seems there were sides to Tim I never knew, and I'll just have to accept that, hard though it might be. Let's put it aside and raise our glasses to Tim.'

We toasted the lad. I was glad she had decided to move on, if surprised at the suddenness of it.

'Everything going alright with you?' I asked.

'Life is good.'

'You're a lot more upbeat than the last time we spoke.'

'Am I not allowed to be?'

'Of course you are. I'm delighted to see it.'

'Sometimes good things happen when you least expect them to.'

'Now you're being cryptic.'

'No. Just careful. Maybe I don't want to jinx it.'

At that moment George Taylor walked in, saw me and waved.

'That's my cue to leave you to it,' Maura said.

'You're in a hurry.'

I knew Maura was shy and tended not to be good when she met people unexpectedly or out of context, but this seemed abrupt, even for her.

'Oh, I have to meet someone.'

'Anyone I know?'

'I don't think so,' Maura said briskly, and whisked out.

I watched her, wondering what had changed for my friend, but figuring that whatever it was could only be positive.

'Hope I didn't interrupt anything,' George said as he sat down in the seat Maura had just vacated.

'Not at all. I'd like your opinion on something, actually.'

It occurred to me that George Taylor had either taught or been principal to the children of almost every family in Garshaigh and its environs for the past three decades. If anyone knew who Thomas was or where he might have come from, George would. Explaining the confidential nature of what I was about to say, I told him the strange story of Gregory and his disappearances, my initial, albeit incorrect, reading of the situation, and my visit to Garda Doyle that afternoon.

George sipped his ale and scratched his head.

'Well, well,' he said. 'That's an odd one, isn't it?'

'It is an unusual case.'

'If I didn't know better, I'd say you have just stepped into the middle of a local legend.'

'Explain,' I said, puzzled.

'There is a folk tale, of sorts, hereabouts. A kind of urban – or should I say *rural* – myth. It tells of a young mother who becomes pregnant through incest – by her father, if I remember the details correctly. Terrified of being discovered, he takes her into the woods and locks her in a cabin he has constructed there. He brings her food and water, and when she comes to full term, she gives birth to a little boy.'

The shadows had grown long in the pub. I could hear the murmur of conversation around us, and smell alcohol and a faint under-scent of smoke and burning turf. It was a pleasant place to be and a pity that we were talking about such dark matters.

'The father knows he will be undone if he is ever found out – Ireland back then was still in the throes of church tyranny, and there was the criminal element of it all – so he insists she remain in the woods to raise the child. He still brings out parcels of food, but by now his visits have grown very short, and often he does not bother to come for days at a time, and the mother and her boy grow hungry and desperate. Gradually, owing to the loneliness and the trauma of her abuse, she begins to go insane. She takes to roaming the woodland paths, taking the child with her, and day by day ventures deeper and deeper into the forest. One morning her father arrives at the cabin to find it empty. Day after day he searches for the girl, and they do say he finally found her, half-dead from hunger and cold by a grove of willows near the lower slopes of the mountains.'

'And the child?'

'She was cradling him in her arms, but he had died during the night, of exposure.'

I shuddered involuntarily, then got us two more drinks.

'What has that to do with Gregory and Thomas?' I asked when I returned to our table.

'Bear with me. I can't say for certain, but I believe the events I have just recounted happened, if they really happened at all, in the late 1970s or early 1980s. The story began to receive general circulation around 1985. It was timely, I suppose, what with the Kerry Babies case beginning to creep into the headlines.

'People have always said that parts of the woods are haunted. Of course, the details of these ghostly occurrences were non-specific, but around late 1989 when I started work here, I began hearing tales of this type. Hikers would say they had seen the figure of a child through the trees, or heard the sound of a baby crying.'

I felt a slight tremor of unease at that, recalling my own experience while hiking with George.

'Now you're scaring me. You know I thought I heard that when we were hiking last summer.'

'I generally don't pay much heed to such things. People from Parks and Wildlife have spoken of finding trails of small footprints that lead to impassable thickets, vanishing into trees no one – not even a child – could penetrate.'

'Ghosts don't leave footprints,' I said dryly.

'There are strange things in those woods,' George said, but would be drawn no further on the subject.

19

A large bunch of flowers were delivered to the school's staff room for Maura the next day. Flushing a beetroot red, she took the offering and scuttled back to her seat. I ran into her in the school library a little while later.

'So who's the lucky guy?' I asked.

'I don't know what you mean,' she said half-heartedly, clearly bursting to tell me.

'Oh, I think you do,' I said, playing along. 'Teachers get bunches of shrubbery like that, in my experience, if they are retiring or if they have admirers. Now, unless you are a lot older than you seem …'

'Yes, I've met someone,' Maura said, the delight obvious in her voice.

'Anyone I know?'

'I doubt it. He doesn't live in Garshaigh, and he's not a teacher.'

'I do have interests outside of my work you know,' I said.

'Of course you do. It's just, well, he's not really like anyone I've ever met before.'

'I do believe you are quite smitten, Maura. Good for you. Do you think I might get to meet this charming new beau any time soon?'

'Let's wait and see. Like I said, I don't want to put a hex on anything. I've had terrible luck with blokes in the past, and I do *really* like this one. I'm trying to take it slowly. Not seem too needy.'

'Judging by the flowers, your approach appears to be working,' I said, giving her a thumbs up. 'And don't sell yourself short. I'm sure he is just as nervous about having such an amazing woman in his life as you are about being with him.'

'D'you think?'

'Well, he certainly isn't concerned about public displays of affection. I'd guess he is telling you pretty loud and clear that he's into you.'

'He is, isn't he?' Maura said, not even trying to suppress a smile.

Later that day I was having a cup of coffee in the staff room. Maura had put her gift in some water in a vase and left it on the windowsill above the sink. I was rinsing out my mug, thinking about Gregory and the story George Taylor had told me, not really focusing on where I was or what I was doing, when my eye fixed on a small card amid the foliage. It was attached to one of those plastic sticks florists use for just that purpose. It had a short message written on it in block capitals, and in a moment of horror I recognised the script: TO MAURA, IN HONOUR OF OUR TWO WEEK ANNIVERSARY. WITH LOVE, R. I put down my mug and looked closely at the card. The writing did look very like the notes I had been receiving, but then it's hard to tell with block capitals, and I am certainly not a handwriting expert. 'R' could refer to any name that began with that letter – Rory, Ryan or Robert. I saw from the watermark on the card that the flowers had been ordered from Liz's, a flower shop in the town. Of course, I could just do the sensible thing and ask Maura if her new boyfriend was a psychotic ex-convict. What could she possibly find offensive about such an interrogation? And the flower shop would probably (quite rightly) refuse to give me any information on who had ordered the bouquet for Maura – it was, after all, none of my business.

Deciding that I was getting far too paranoid for my own good, I pushed the idea out of my mind and went back to class.

20

Gregory Finnegan sat opposite me in Carla's, Garshaigh's finest café, eating a large ice-cream sundae. He had already managed to get most of it all over his face. He looked as if he was thoroughly enjoying himself, though, so I made no comment; I just sat and picked through a fruit plate I had bought, which was proving to be far less appetising than the creamy, chocolate treat my young friend was wolfing down.

'Shane,' Gregory said out of the blue.

'Yeah?'

'Who are *The A-Team*?'

I thought about that.

'D'you mean the Ed Sheeran song?'

'No. I think it's a TV show.'

I grinned. This was a blast from the past. I had watched the

1980s action series as a child and, like most people of my vintage, had very fond memories of it. But I doubted Gregory was talking about that.

'I think you must mean the film – there was a movie released with that name a couple of years ago. It was based on an old show that was out when I was your age.'

'No – this is a programme tha's on every week. Thomas watches it.'

'Does he?' I asked, interested now, as this had been my primary reason for the trip out for ice-cream: I have found that it often acts as a wonderful conduit for conversation with kids.

'Yeah. He says he really likes it. I axed my Mammy 'bou' it, but she looked on the TV planner and she couldn' find it.'

'It does get repeated sometimes, but to be honest I haven't seen it in a while. You sure Thomas watches it?'

'Yeah. I was telling him 'bou' *Power Rangers*, and he din't know 'bou' them at all. I axed him what was his fav'rite show, an' he said "*The A-Team*". He said … ,' Gregory paused, thinking for a moment, '… he said he "pities the fool who doesn' like it too".'

I guffawed aloud to hear my young friend echo Mr T's (one of the show's iconic stars) catchphrases.

'Really? What else does Thomas like?'

'Well, he doesn' like the Xbox neither. An' he don' have a PlayStation.'

'No? Well I suppose some kids survive without them.'

'I don' know any other kids who don' have one or th'other.'

'Does he play any games?'

'He says he has a … a … Specky or something.'

'A Specky?' I paused, my mind whirling. 'You don't mean a Spectrum? A ZX Spectrum?'

'Yeah, that's it. Is that some new kind of console?'

'No, it's really, really old. I used to have one, *that's* how ancient it is. It's what we used to call a home computer. It was made in England by a company called Sinclair.'

The ZX Spectrum was invented in the early 1980s by Sir Clive Sinclair, a mercurial but brilliant British scientist. It was a hugely idiosyncratic piece of engineering, beautifully designed but blessed with foam keys and a minuscule memory; that did not stop it becoming hugely popular, introducing a generation of young people to the joys of programming. It also spawned thousands of games of varying degrees of quality and not a little strangeness – the Spectrum was a very English phenomenon, so you were as likely to come across a video game inspired by the *Carry On* films as you were to encounter an alien shoot-'em-up.

'He says he plays *Manic Miner* and *Skool Daze*. They is his fav'rites.'

Once again I could not help myself from chuckling.

'You can't be serious! He really plays those? His mum or dad must have an old machine in their house, because you can't buy Spectrums in the shops anymore, and those games are, like, really, *really* old. I used to play them when I was a kid – I loved *Manic Miner*, I think that one was my favourite. You used to buy them on cassettes.'

'On *what*?'

'Like a tape.'

Gregory looked at me blankly, and I realised we were talking about technology so far removed from his experience as to be alien. Yet his best friend was obviously familiar with it. I was struck again by how bizarre that was.

'Doesn't matter. Those games were great fun. You could play them for weeks and weeks and still find new stuff in them.'

'What's *Manic Miner* like?'

'Well, I suppose it's a little bit similar to *Super Mario Brothers*. You have to climb ladders and jump over things. But it was made when video games were only just starting out, so I think *you* would probably think it was very slow and not really exciting.'

'Thomas says it's the best.'

'Your friend seems to be a very unusual kid. I'd love to meet him.'

Gregory shook his head.

'He don' like adults.'

'Why not?'

'Says they bad. I tole him my mammy was nice. But he din't b'lieve me.'

'Your mum tells me you haven't gone out at night since the police found you.'

'I can't get out no more. Mammy locked the door and hid the keys. She put a thing on it that locks, too, high up so I couldn' reach it. I'm good at findin' the keys, but that new thing was too hard for me.'

'So you haven't seen Thomas then?'

'No. I sees him.'

'How?'

'He comes in my room now.'

I felt something icy shoot up my back, fingers of dread creeping along my spine.

'How does he get in if the door is locked?'

'I don't know. I wake up an' he's there.'

'Do you let him in the window?'

'He just a little kid. He couldn' climb in no window.'

And that seemed to be that.

When I dropped Gregory back home, though, I talked to Orla about these night-time visitations.

'Not possible,' she said. 'Like you suggested, I've put a monitor in his room. The only thing it has shown me is that Greg has started talking in his sleep.'

'You've heard him talking?'

'Yeah, but not conversations. Gibberish. You know how people talk nonsense when they're asleep.'

'You're sure it's just him? There's no way this kid might have sneaked in?'

'I have the keys to the house in my bedside locker. Unless he's some kind of cat burglar, he's not getting in.'

I thought it might be interesting to try and find an old Spectrum but, try as I might, I couldn't source one locally, and ordering online would have taken longer than I was prepared to wait. I compromised by finding a Spectrum emulator application that I could download to my laptop, and also managed to get digital copies of the games Gregory had mentioned. To my great surprise there was quite a large community of Spectrum fans online, who were more than happy to discuss their passion and help me out.

Getting a boxset of the original 1980s *A-Team* series was much easier, and one afternoon the following week Gregory, Millie (I had brought her along with me once, and she and Gregory had hit it off so well, I decided to make a habit of taking her on my visits) and I had a nostalgia-fuelled hour in which we watched an episode of the series. The team were hired to vanquish an evil business tycoon and his small army of thugs who were holding a desert town to ransom – they achieved this, or so it seemed to me, by driving very fast around dusty streets in their van while shooting randomly out the door with their machine guns, throwing thugs bodily over the bonnets of their cars, and then getting themselves locked up in a shed conveniently full of all the equipment and materials needed to build a makeshift tank, which they then used to escape and bludgeon their foes into submission. During all this, no one ever got badly hurt and everyone, even the baddies, seemed to be having a rare old time. Then we played the delightfully retro games on my laptop, which I attached up to Gregory's television set to give us something close to the original experience.

Gregory was fascinated by it all. He did seem to get a little bored in the middle of the *A-Team* episode, but when the final showdown occurred, he got very excited, jumping up and down on the couch and throwing punches in the air. The games, with their quaint, blocky graphics and hugely simplistic sounds had a strange effect on him – it was almost as if he was looking at a museum exhibit.

'This the games you played when you was a kid?'

'Well, I did other stuff too – I wasn't allowed play computer games all day – but I would have spent a bit of time with *Manic Miner* and *Skool Daze*, yes.'

'It's so … so different to the PlayStation.'

'Yeah, it is, isn't it? Games have changed a lot. The amount of computer memory they used to make a game like *Manic Miner*, which is really big – I mean, it's got twenty or so different levels to it – would really be just a tiny, tiny fraction of the memory in a cheap phone today.'

Gregory made the little figure jump over a simply rendered digital duck, which was flapping towards him on the screen.

'Greg, has Thomas even heard of the PlayStation?'

Engrossed as he was in the game, the boy shrugged and made a non-committal sound.

'Seriously, do you get the impression he even knows what you're talking about when you mention, I dunno, *Grand Theft Auto* or *Tour of Duty*?'

His final computer-generated miner killed, Gregory looked at me thoughtfully.

'He don' wanna talk abou' it. This is good though – him 'n' me can chat abou' the Spectrum now.'

I watched him play for a while longer, then it was time to go home. As I was leaving, a thought occurred to me, and I stuck my head back into the living room.

'Gregory, will you do something for me?'

He looked up at me expectantly.

'Next time you see Thomas, will you ask him what song is number one in the charts?'

'What charts?'

'I think he'll know what I'm talking about. Just ask him, would you? Please? It'd help me to understand things better.'

Shaking his head as if I was a bit simple and needed to be humoured, Gregory agreed.

I had a suspicion I knew what he would tell me.

21

I ran into Tim Fox's mother by accident at a local history festival I was covering for the newspaper. She was one of three women who had been employed to serve tea to the milling crowds who had come to take a look at Sliabh Gullion, a large Victorian house on the outskirts of the town. Once the seat of an Anglo-Irish family who were large farmers in the area, it had just been opened to the public. The local historical society had decided to mark the event by organising a series of tours and lectures using the manor as a starting point, and I had been asked to go along and write something to commemorate the event.

A marquee had been set up on the lawn, where visitors could buy tea, coffee and cakes, and after a couple of hours taking in the ornately decorated rooms and chatting with the owners, I repaired there for some refreshment.

Having never met Biddy Fox before, I had no idea that the person pouring my coffee was the mother of the young man who had taken up so much of my time lately, and therefore was surprised when she introduced herself.

'Maura tells me you've been very helpful with findin' out what happened to my Timmy,' she said as I shook her hand. She looked to be in her late forties, and that she had lived every day of that time as hard as she could – her face was a network of deep lines and her reddish hair was shot through with streaks of grey and white.

I had not been expecting to be faced with a grieving parent that day, and was unprepared. 'But I'm not sure how much help I've really been,' I said, more than a little uncomfortable. 'I can only tell you how sorry I am for your loss.'

'It's just nice to know someone cares about him enough to try,' she said. 'I really appreciate it.'

A queue was forming behind me, but she seemed oblivious to it.

'He was a good lad, was Timmy. Never gave me any trouble. Always tried to do his best for his old mam.'

'That's nice,' I said, for want of anything else to say.

'They locked him up but he never done nothin' wrong.'

'Well, I don't think he deserved to be locked up, Mrs Fox, but he did have a lot of unpaid parking fines,' I said. 'So, while the punishment didn't fit the crime—'

'You sayin' my lad was a criminal?' she shot back, bristling immediately.

'No. Of course not. It was a terrible mistake, from what I can tell.'

'Because if you are, I'm here to tell you that you are wrong!' she continued as if I hadn't spoken.

'I have only heard good things about Tim,' I said, acutely aware now of the shuffling of feet behind me as the line of thirsty historians got ever more restless.

'What them fellas said about him, that was all lies,' she said more gently, her anger dissipating as quickly as it had flared.

'You've lost me, Mrs Fox. I never heard anyone saying anything about Tim other than what a sweet kid he was.'

'Said he was dealin' drugs or some nonsense,' Biddy said as if to herself.

'Who said that?' I asked.

'No one.' She was staring into space now.

I took my coffee.

'Are you okay, Mrs Fox?'

She looked up as if she was surprised I was still there.

'I'm grand,' she said, smiling suddenly. 'Have a nice afternoon now.'

And then she was talking to the person behind me, and I might as well have not been there at all. I left her to it, wondering about the conversation we had just had and what it all meant.

22

St Smoling's had a staff night out before the mid-term break at Halloween, which involved the assembled teaching staff having dinner in the small restaurant above Stanbridge's, and then convening for drinks in the bar below. We all had a grand old time during the meal, everyone agreeing that shop talk was completely off limits. By the time we got down to the main drinking area, everyone was full and happy, and George Taylor was keeping us all entertained by playing Beatles songs on an old upright piano which the landlord kept for occasions like these.

George had just struck up the opening to 'Penny Lane' and we were all joining in enthusiastically when the door to the pub swung open and Rex Gifford strode in. I froze. He seemed to be headed in my direction, and I was ready to defend myself in whatever way was required. To my great surprise, however, rather than marching straight up to me, he veered off to my left and threw his arms around Maura, who reciprocated his advances with genuine affection.

'Everyone, this is Rex,' she said when the pair had broken their embrace.

'So this is the guy you've been hiding from us,' Davina, one of the school secretaries, said.

'Have you been keeping my identity from these good people?' Gifford asked, looking at Maura with mock concern.

'Maybe I wanted to have you all to myself,' Maura said, looking embarrassed but delighted.

The group milled about, introducing themselves. Gifford was his charming self, expressing interest in every one of them, asking about the subjects they taught and, as usual, showing more than a passing familiarity with the intricacies and difficulties incumbent on each. I hung back, which was easy to do unnoticed among such a bustling and noisy crowd. I was feeling sick to my stomach and furious that I had not acted on my instincts and investigated Maura's new-found love interest when I had been tempted to.

The evening began to take on a sluggish, nightmare-like quality. George continued to play the piano, but the music sounded discordant and the surreal lyrics of Lennon and McCartney felt sinister. I watched Gifford closely as he laughed and chatted with my friends and colleagues, convivial and witty. Once, he caught me watching him and flashed me a toothy grin, his face full of good humour. I did not respond, just stared back blankly.

Finally Maura got up and began to make her way towards the bathrooms, and I took my chance, pushing my way quickly through the crowd to cut her off before she got to the door.

'I need a word,' I said, steering her to the end of the bar.

I could see Gifford, who was deep in conversation with one of our group, watching me in his peripheral vision, but I didn't care.

'What's up?' Maura asked.

'Your friend is not who you think he is.'

'Really?' Her voice took on a harder tone. 'And who do I think he is?'

'He was in prison,' I said.

'I know. He told me. You should know better than anyone that doesn't make you a bad person.'

'Do you know what he was in prison for?'

'He told me he didn't do it.'

'Do you know what he was sentenced for, Maura?'

'No, and I don't want to know. I told Rex that it isn't important to me. If Tim's situation has taught me anything, it's that the legal system in this country does not work, that the people caught up in it are, more often than not, innocent victims of an outmoded, Victorian mechanism that serves only to protect the status quo.'

'Jesus, Maura, you sound just like Gifford. Did he say all that crap? Sure, Tim Fox got a raw deal, but believe me, there are plenty of people in jail because society needs to be protected from them. And that man over there is a perfect example – he should not be walking around free and you should not be in his company.'

'He told me there would be people who would try and turn me against him,' Maura said, looking hurt and angry now. 'I just never thought it would be you.'

'He preys on women, Maura. He's a sick, sadistic but very smart man, and there is something badly wrong with him. Please believe me. You need to get away from him. Right now, if possible.'

'I am happy for the first time in a very long while, Shane. Have you any idea how lonely I have been? Why do you think I dedicate so much of my life – my *whole* life, if I'm honest – to my job? It's because I don't have anything else. Now I do, and you want me to give it up.'

'I do. I'm sorry, Maura, but I want you to get away from this man. Rex Gifford is dangerous on a level that is difficult to comprehend. If you continue to spend time with him, he will hurt you. Badly. Not maybe, not possibly, but definitely.'

'Why are you being so mean?' she asked, tears coming into her voice now. 'I was having such a lovely evening.'

'I wish you could see that I'm not being cruel. I'm doing this because I care about you, and I know that man all too well. There is no happy way for this to end. I wish there was. I'm sorry, Maura, but Rex Gifford is a sociopathic sex offender, a violent criminal.'

'You are a cold-hearted bastard,' Maura said. Turning, she fled through the door that led to the toilets. I looked over and Gifford was standing slightly away from the group, his hands in his pockets, smiling at me. When Maura came out five minutes later, they left together. I had done my best, but it wasn't good enough.

Rex Gifford was way ahead of me, and I was out of ideas.

23

I couldn't sleep that night, and dawn found me and Millie walking on the beach as I tried to make sense of what had happened the night before; I strove desperately to think of a way to do something – anything – to fix it.

There was no doubt in my mind that Gifford was sending me a clear message: he could get to me if he so wished, and there was nothing I could do to stop him. I found myself wondering if I should just walk away from this – Maura was an adult, and I had warned her in no uncertain terms about what she was getting into. While Gifford scared me, I thought I could probably handle him in a physical confrontation, and I was determined to be more careful in future about getting usable evidence if he came anywhere near me. I had made a complaint to the police already, and I would pursue that complaint without hesitation given the opportunity.

The problem was his determination to hurt me through others. Millie had been poisoned, and Maura was his next target.

I was in no doubt that Gifford had told her, probably through a mist of crocodile tears, that he had been unjustly imprisoned. I could guess his version of the Hayley Porter story, a telling of events that cast him as the autistic girl's only loyal friend. I would have bet he claimed he was framed by a crooked police force backed up by a complacent social service team, all of whom simply wanted the case closed and had scapegoated this gentle, mildly eccentric guy who worked in the local café.

Maura certainly believed she knew who Rex Gifford was. She thought he was a decent, good-hearted man who had been treated unfairly by a system designed to devour the weak and disenfranchised. And her experience with Tim had made her easy prey.

I paused and looked out at the waves. The sky was a blend of pink and light blue as the disc of the sun slowly dragged itself above the horizon. To my left a ringed plover scuttled here and there, foraging for crustaceans in the wet sand below the waterline. In the trees that loomed over the dunes a long-eared owl hooted its farewell to the night.

I had found such a peaceful place to live, somewhere I really felt I could settle down and build a life. Yet my past and the pain that seemed to orbit it had followed me here, drawn to it like vultures to carrion.

Maybe I was not meant to be at ease.

I walked slowly to the dunes and sat, resting my back on the cool sand. Millie watched me for a second and then continued to snuffle about here and there.

The idea of simply letting events play out seemed attractive. Why should I exhaust myself rushing around trying to clean up this mess when no one seemed to want me to? Gifford would do whatever the hell he wanted regardless of my actions anyway.

But what if that involved hurting Maura? Could I live with that on my conscience?

I suddenly felt worn out, so tired that all I wanted to do was to stay lying right where I was and sleep. But I knew I couldn't. In fact, I was no longer confused about what I needed to do.

It was time Rex Gifford and I had another talk. And this time, I was going to be far less restrained.

24

It didn't take me very long to find him this time – it occurred to me that he might have wanted (or at least expected) me to come looking, and so chose to remain in plain sight. At any rate, when I arrived at the café where he and I had last talked, Rex Gifford was sitting in exactly the same spot, an empty mug in front of him and a large, heavy book open on the table.

As usual he looked fresh and genial, smiling indulgently at me as I sat down across from him. I still had not slept and was wearing the same clothes I had on the day before, and must have presented a rumpled, gaunt figure, but he made no comment.

'It's good to see you, Shane,' he said, closing the tome he had been reading – I saw it was a book about sustainable energy.

'We need to talk,' I said.

A waitress came down and I ordered coffee.

'Why do we need to talk?' Rex Gifford countered. 'What, in fact, do we need to converse about that has not already been said between us?'

'Maura. I want you to leave her alone. Your argument, or whatever this is, is with me. She has done nothing to harm you and is no threat to any mayhem you're planning to do now you have your freedom.'

'You do me a disservice. I bear Ms Bellamy no ill will. I like her very much, in fact. We are kindred spirits, you see.'

I blinked at that.

'How so?'

'We have both been wounded by the slings and arrows of outrageous fortune.'

I had to stifle a laugh. 'In very different ways. Maura has been hurt through seeing people she cared about and tried to help let down by the system. Any unhappiness you might feel is purely the result of your own actions.'

'How do you know I didn't have an abusive, neglectful childhood? I may be the result of societal forces far beyond my control.'

I sighed. 'I don't really care anymore, Rex. What do you want from me? Do you want to hear me say you've won? That I have been bettered by you? Fine. If it makes you go away and leave my friends alone, I'll gladly say it.'

'I don't think it's about winning or losing, Shane. You do have a simplistic view of things, don't you?'

'Explain it to me then.'

'You wouldn't understand.'

I leaned in close to him. I could see that he had purple flecks in his green eyes, which were full of something I could not discern. 'If you do not leave Maura Bellamy alone, if you harm her in even the slightest manner, I will see to it that you suffer. The prison sentence you got before, that'll be nothing. Like you have been at pains to point out, I'm not a social care worker, so I am not tied by the constraints I was when we last met.'

'What are you saying?' Rex asked, grinning broadly.

I shook my head, stood up and left.

The street was busy outside, and it wasn't difficult to lose myself amid the milling crowd. I moved quickly up the thoroughfare, then doubled back and found a position in a doorway across from the café where Gifford was still sitting, once again engrossed in his book. I waited.

An hour passed. Through the window I could see Gifford order another cup of coffee. My stomach rumbled with hunger and my nerves with anxiety and exhaustion. I waited.

Another forty-five minutes ground by. At one point I found myself starting to nod off on my feet and came back to consciousness with a start. Luckily Gifford was still in his position opposite me, and I was able to stamp my feet and get the blood circulating again.

As morning became afternoon the object of my attentions stood up, took the volume he had been studying and left the café, heading at a brisk pace up the street in the direction of the university. I followed.

He walked with his head down and a set of expensive-looking earphones, the big ones that look like they belong in a sound studio, covering his ears. After a mile or so he turned onto a residential street, and I knew this would have to be my chance or I would lose him. The houses there had large gardens with mature trees and high hedges – perfect cover. I could see no one on either side of the road:

people here were either at work or having extended lunches. And if they weren't, I was close to just not caring.

I sped my pace to a run, came up behind, grabbed him by the scruff of the neck, and dragged him into an open gateway and behind a high wall before he knew what had happened.

My plan had been to get the drop on him and, aided by the element of surprise, deliver a moderate beating. It was not an elegant plan, and it was not a particularly well-formed one, but it was all my addled brain could come up with.

And it did not work.

Before I had a chance to draw my fist back to deliver a blow, Gifford swung his heavy book around and slammed it into the side of my head, stunning me and sending me reeling sideways. I did not fall, but I was driven into the trunk of an elm tree, and all the breath exploded from my lungs. To my credit, I did try to throw a couple of half-hearted punches into the air I thought my opponent was occupying, but this was met with a fierce blow to my ribs, and I sagged.

It took me a good ten seconds to regain any kind of composure, and I opened my eyes expecting to find Gifford standing over me, gleeful in his victory. To my surprise, what I saw instead was his back as he walked briskly out the gate, leaving me bruised, embarrassed and deflated. I had just made a complete idiot of myself, and things were, if anything, worse than before.

All in all, not a great morning's work.

DR B: So you did lose control.

SD: In an attempt to *gain* control over the situation, yes. It was a very stupid thing to do.

DR B: He bested you.

SD: He kicked my ass. I never saw it coming. I had always assumed he was a physical coward – common knowledge suggests men who prey on women always are. I thought I could give him a hiding, warn him to never lay a hand on Maura again, and everything would be hunky-dory.

DR B: It's almost a childish response to the problem, isn't it?

SD: A little bit, yeah. You hit my friend, so I'm going to beat you up.

DR B: How did you feel about him getting the better of you?

SD: Are you asking me if I felt emasculated?

DR B: Did you?

SD: Completely. I felt like a sissy. I had sailed out there to try and defend Maura and all I ended up doing was looking like an ass.

DR B: How important was it that you defended Maura's honour?

SD: Making her safe was uppermost in my mind, obviously, but honour was in there somewhere too.

DR B: Your code had been violated.

SD: Yes.

DR B: How quaint.

SD: Are you making fun of me now, Doctor?

DR B: Not at all. I think it is quite admirable what you were trying to do, although I feel it was very misguided and misplaced, and we are running up against machismo and a hero complex again. But your heart was in the right place.

SD: Thanks. I think.

25

I drove home feeling intermittently sorry for myself and just plain angry at my stupidity, not to mention my ineffectiveness. I had been arrogant and foolish, and I somehow knew the fallout would be dire. Despite the abundant self-recrimination, however, I fell onto my bed and slept for six hours straight. I was awakened by the sound of my phone ringing, and I fumbled for it drowsily.

'Yeah.'

'Shane, it's Orla Finnegan.'

'Hello, Orla.'

'I'm sorry to call you so late.'

'What time is it?'

'It's about eleven, I think.'

I rubbed my eyes with the heel of my hand.

'No … um … that's fine, Orla. Is everything okay?'

'I don't know. Can you come out? I hate to ask but I'm … I'm frightened.'

I stood and looked about for my boots, then realised I hadn't taken them off when I had flung myself down on the bed. I walked into the bathroom and, glancing in the mirror, saw that I looked decidedly rumpled. A purple bruise had blossomed on the left side of my face, but I reckoned I was more or less presentable.

'I'll be there as quickly as I can. Has somebody tried to break in or something? Are the kids alright?'

'I don't know. Just get here, please.'

'Should I call the police?'

'I don't think they can help with this.'

I didn't know what to say to that, so I just told her to sit tight and got moving.

She met me at the door looking scared half to death.

'What's going on, Orla?'

'Come in. Quickly.'

I did, following her into the kitchen. She had an old-fashioned tape cassette recorder sitting on the table.

'Do you know how to use one of these?' she asked.

'I do.'

'Listen to the tape.'

I sat down and pressed play. At first all the machine played was a hiss of ambient noise. Then, amid the crackling, I heard voices. It was difficult to make out words, at first.

'What am I listening to?'

'What I heard on the baby monitor this evening.'

I shot her a glance.

'So this was going on in Gregory's room?'

She nodded.

'Why didn't you call me right away?'

'I think I was frightened you would tell me what I was hearing is real.'

I strained to hear.

'Are there two voices or is he talking to himself?'

'Just listen,' Orla said, almost in a whisper.

I picked up the machine and put it close to my ear. I closed my eyes, letting the sound wash over me.

I don't want to go out th' window. Gregory's voice. He sounded upset.

I want to play in the trees. Another child's voice, but lower in register. Perhaps older.

Mammy doesn't want me goin' no more. She says it dangerous.

This room is too small. Outside you can hide and I can look for you.

'Do you recognise the other voice?'

She shook her head, her eyes wide and glassy. The tape continued.

We could go out the door. The deeper voice.

I tole you – I don't gots the key.

We could find it.

No. Mammy gets scairt when I goes off with you. It makes her cry.

But I cry when you won't come and play with me! There was an urgency. An anger.

We can play somethin' in here. Anythin' you want.

The tape lapsed back to the hiss.

'Could it be Gregory dreaming? Making the two voices in his sleep?' Orla asked.

'I don't know if people do that,' I admitted.

'Maybe he's just playing. He could be doing it when he's awake.'

I'm going. I don't like it in here.

Will you come back and see me?

You come and see me next time.

Tha's hard for me.

You has to play fair. Next time is your turn.

There was a thudding sound, as if something was being moved, then more banging and Orla's voice:

Gregory, are you alright? Gregory, love …

'He was in the room by himself, sitting on the floor,' she said, her face deathly white.

'So there was no other kid?'

'The window was open, and there was old pine needles and dirt on the mat. I looked out the window and I thought …'

She paused, biting her lip.

'What?'

'I thought I saw a child, a little boy, walking away into the trees beyond the fence.'

I switched off the tape with a click.

'Could a small kid have got up and through the window? And been able to get down again?'

'I don't know.'

'What did the child look like?'

'Just an outline. A shadow, really. I think I saw him … I don't know anymore.'

'Did you look for tracks?'

'I was too scared to go out.'

I nodded and got up, switching on the torch on my phone as I went. The trip proved futile. I scanned the area below the window, but it had been relatively dry that day, and there were no signs I could discern. A drainpipe did run close by the window, but there were no footholds, so it would be a treacherous climb. I went back inside and told Orla.

'I'm going to record the tape on my phone, and I'll play it to the police,' I said.

'What should I do?'

'Bolt the window shut. A simple screw through the latch will do it. If there is a visitor, that'll keep him out.'

The woman nodded, holding herself tightly.

'He seems to be saying he's not coming back.'

'Or that he wants Gregory to go to him.'

'We'll just have to make sure that doesn't happen,' I said.

Famous last words.

26

I called in to see Harry at the police station the following morning, thinking that he should know about Gregory's visitor. I played him the recording I had made of the tape – the sound quality was even worse than the original, but I watched the young man's eyes grow wide as he listened.

'Is this real?' he asked when it was over.

'There was mud and pine needles on the rug, as if someone who had been trudging around the woods was there. I didn't find any tracks outside, but that doesn't mean anything.'

'This is really weird,' Harry said, not looking happy at all.

'I just thought I'd let you know.'

I stood to leave, then stopped as a thought occurred to me.

'Harry, does the name Tim Fox ring any bells?'

He looked up at me sharply.

'Yeah. What's your connection to the Foxes?'

'You know Tim's dead?'

'Yeah, I'd heard that.'

'I'm looking into the circumstances of his demise. A friend, one of his old teachers, asked me to do it, see what we can learn. She feels she let him down.'

Harry nodded and sighed deeply.

'You know, he wasn't a bad kid. Confused, I suppose.'

'He had a learning difficulty, and some literacy issues, yeah.'

'Not what I mean. I always thought he was a very angry guy.'

'Really? How so?'

'He was what you might call "known to the gardaí".'

'It's the first I've heard of it.'

'He was never prosecuted, not until that final time. He tended to play the handicapped card when he got in a tight spot.'

'I don't think they use that word anymore.'

'You know what I mean,' Harry said, brushing off my rebuke. 'He always let on he didn't know he'd done anything wrong, or that he couldn't understand what was being said to him. We generally just let him off.'

'What kind of things brought him to your attention?'

'Petty stuff generally. Fighting, drunk and disorderly, disturbing the peace. He was caught with a slightly larger quantity of a controlled substance than could be easily explained, but even that was confiscated and he walked away. I'll be straight with you, I thought he should have gone down for it, but the lads took pity on him. He had the ability to seem just a simple, harmless, slightly scatter-brained youngster who kept on getting into trouble through no fault of his own.'

'But you're not convinced.'

'No. The incidents of trouble were too consistent.'

'Couldn't he have just fallen in with a bad crowd? He made an easy scapegoat, after all.'

'No. I saw him with his crew – he wasn't the butt of any jokes, or the weaker one they pushed around. If anything, he was someone they looked up to.'

I sat back and pondered that for a moment. Had I been all wrong in my approach to this young man? I had to find out.

'Could I talk to any of these friends of Tim's?'

'Why?'

'It's a perspective I haven't come in contact with yet. I'd bought into the idea of him being a friendless character, at the mercy of others and adrift in the world. It never even occurred to me that he would have a gang of cronies.'

'Well, there you have it,' Harry said. 'I don't want to be bad-mouthing the lad and him dead and all ...'

'I'm not suggesting you are. Who of these friends was he closest to?'

'I couldn't tell you.'

'Make an educated guess.'

'You're not going to go stirring up more trouble for yourself now, are you? These are not nice people.' Harry's voice took on a more firm tone.

'All I want to do is ask about Tim. Get their sense of him.'

'Things have been a lot quieter around here since Tim Fox went inside. I know he was put away for parking tickets, but I don't think his old crew ever really got that. They've all kept their heads down since.'

'I promise I won't set off any bad behaviour. Just give me a name.'

'Try Pat Johnson. He lives out on the ring road, in that old thatched cottage.'

'Thanks, Harry.'

'Don't make me regret telling you.'

I smiled and left, assuring Harry that nothing bad would come of my investigations. I had nothing if not good intentions.

27

I had driven past the cottage many times but, in that way we have with the familiar, had never really looked at it. I saw as I got out of the Skoda that it was bordering on the derelict: the thatch was grey-brown and filthy, the windows green with moss and the small garden out front overgrown and beset with weeds.

I knocked on the door and waited, then knocked again. I could hear the sounds of a TV or radio playing somewhere inside the small structure and thought I would try my chances around the back. This proved harder than I had expected, as the vegetation had completely taken over the small path that led to the rear of the building, but I forced my way through and found what I took to be the back door, rapping smartly on it. A window to my left was flung open, and an unshaven face was thrust out.

'What the fuck do you want?'

'Are you Pat?'

The question seemed to puzzle him. The brow furrowed and the eyes squinted.

'Why d'you wanna know?'

'I'm a friend of Tim Fox's,' I said, figuring it was kind of a lie, but kind of true, too.

The clouds parted, and a smile beamed at me.

'That door don't open so good. Come 'round the front and I'll let ya in.'

The house was as much a mess on the inside as I had expected.

'D'ya want some tae?' my host asked.

'Yeah, thanks,' I said, deciding I would have to brave any health risks such an offer might carry. 'You *are* Pat Johnson, then?'

'Guilty as charged.' My companion punched me on the shoulder, a little harder than I would have liked.

He was a good head and shoulders taller than me and had probably once been quite muscular – now most of that bulk was cloaked in a thick layer of flab, but I could sense that he was still, physically at least, a force to be reckoned with.

'How'd you know Tim, then?' he asked.

'I work at the school.'

'You a teacher, then?'

'Yes.'

'Never went to school that much meself,' Pat said, bringing me into a filthy, cluttered kitchen. 'Let me find a mug.'

'You know, I just had tea,' I said quickly, my bravado leaving me as I saw mould growing on many of the utensils and crockery that lay, unwashed, on various surfaces about the room.

'You sure? I just made some.'

'I'm certain. Don't put yourself out.'

''Kay.'

The huge youngster sat down on a wooden chair that looked like it was under grievous pressure. I couldn't see anywhere to park myself, so I remained standing.

'You living here long?' I asked, trying to make conversation.

'Not really. My ol' mam threw me out a year ago. I din't have no money or nuthin', but she didn' care. My grandad owned this place, and he said I could stay till I gets a job. I still ain't got one, so I'm still here. I think he forgot, so I reckon I can stay 's long as I likes!'

'Pretty sweet,' I said, offering him a thumbs up.

'What'd you say your name was, pal?'

'Shane,' I said.

'So you was a friend of Tim's?'

'Yes. I'm trying to find out about why he died in prison. Everyone I speak to tells me he was very happy, not the kind of person who would kill themselves.'

'Oh, he was happy alright. Most 'o the time.'

There it was again, that darkness that was creeping into the dayglo-coloured picture of Tim Fox I had been sold.

'So there were times he was sad?'

'Everyone gets sad.'

'That's true. But he was sad a lot?'

Pat was struggling with this conversation

'Not a lot. Well … maybe … I don't know.'

'What did he get sad about?'

'Sad ain't right. He useta get mad about stuff.'

'What kind of stuff?'

'Work 'n' that. Or if his mam got too drunk to make his dinner. Or if he had a hangover.'

'So a lot of things made him angry,' I offered.

'S'pose.'

'What was he like when he was upset?'

'I don' remember.'

'But you said he was cross a lot.'

'He wasn't too nice, really. He could get kinda scary.'

'Were you scared of him?'

Pat sat up straighter.

'Naw. Not me, sure he was my mate, so he was. Why would I be scared?'

I nodded. You didn't have to be a Freudian to read between the lines of that statement: Pat, big as he was, had been terrified of Tim.

'You and him got in a bit of trouble, didn't you?'

He narrowed his eyes.

'What kinda trouble you talkin' about?'

'Well, I heard you got in a few fights.'

He seemed to relax.

'Oh, we was always fightin'.'

'Who'd you fight with?'

'Anyone who pissed us off.'

'Really?'

'Oh yeah. I'll tell you, Tim'd be in the pub havin' a coupla pints and he'd just see some fella across the bar, and he'd start eyeballin' him. He'd keep it up until yer man couldn' take it no more, and he'd come over to see what was up with Tim, and then bam! Tim'd pop him one and it'd all blow up. Me 'n' the lads'd have to jump in.'

I laughed along with Pat, although I was thinking that Tim was starting to sound like a bit of an asshole.

'Tim could hold his own, then?'

A puzzled look.

'He was a good fighter.'

'He was. He wasn't a big fella, now, not like me, but he was fast and he was mean. People around here knew not to mess with him.'

We settled into silence for a moment. I was trying to put all the pieces together, and I just couldn't find a way to make them fit. This picture of Tim Fox jarred completely with everything I'd been told before. It made no sense at all.

'Tim liked a few pints, yeah?' I asked.

'Oh he did. He did, yeah.'

'Did he do anything else?'

'Like what?'

'I dunno. Smoke blow? Snort coke? Drop e's?'

'What the fuck is wrong with you?' Pat said, standing up in annoyance. 'Why would you want to know shit like that?'

'They say he died of an overdose, but a lot of people have told me he didn't ever touch anything like that. And then, a few people have said he did … I just want to understand the truth behind his death. I don't want to cause any trouble, Pat. I'm doing this for Tim as much as for anyone else.'

Pat growled and muttered unintelligibly, but sat down again, pouring some more tar-like tea into his mug.

'He did a little grass, yeah, and one time we got some coke, but he went really fuckin' crazy on that. I thought he was gonna kill someone that night.'

'Did he ever sell dope?'

Pat shuffled uncomfortably.

'Maybe a li'l bit. The garage where he worked, one of the fellas who was there would get more than he needed sometimes, and Tim he always had an eye for makin' a few quid. We'd move it an' he let us keep some o' the money.'

'I see.'

'It was only now an' again though.'

'Of course.'

'You won't tell no one, will ya? My ma threw me out when she caught me with some ecstasy tabs, and she'd be real mad if she thought I was sellin' it.'

'I won't tell anyone, Pat.'

'Thanks.'

'I think she's already pretty mad at you, though, isn't she?'

'She started lettin' me bring me washin' home coupla weeks ago.'

'That's a start, I suppose.'

'I don't really want to move back full time, but it'd be nice to go over for me tea and that. I likes havin' me own place.'

'You've got it really nice,' I said.

'I'm livin' the dream, man,' Pat said, and the words rang in my head all the way home.

28

It had been a couple of days since my argument with Maura and I wanted to call on her so I could tell her what I had learned, but I resisted the desire, figuring I had better give her some space. My new information would just have to wait – it wasn't as if anything bad was going to happen through my keeping it to myself – the worst had already befallen Tim Fox. Worried as I was about Maura, I knew her well enough to understand that pushing her would only foster a greater distance between us. I would just have to let this one lie for a bit.

I went home, had some lunch, and then took Millie for a walk. On the way back, I called into the school, knowing I would find George Taylor at the desk in his office. Despite the fact that we were on mid-term, George was a man of habit, and holidays held little attraction for him.

'Can I tempt you with a cup of coffee and a mid-afternoon scone?' I asked, once Millie and I had knocked and been granted entry to his inner sanctum.

'No, thank you,' George said, pushing a pile of papers aside and adjusting his glasses on his nose.

'You know what all work and no play does, don't you?' I asked.

'It ensures everything is ready and shipshape for when students and staff return next week,' George said, smiling, but firm. 'Now, is there something you two wanted?'

'Just a social call, George.'

'How about a drink later?'

'I could do that.'

'Before you go, I have something for you.'

Reaching onto a shelf behind him, George pulled down a slim folder and tossed it to me.

'What's this?'

'It's another aspect to your ghost story.'

'Really?'

'Take it away and read it. I'll see you later. Stanbridge's at eight sharp?'

'Right you be. Come on, Millie. We know when we're not wanted.'

When I got home I put some water in a bowl for Millie, made myself some tea and then sat down at my kitchen table and opened the folder my friend had given me. It contained three sheets of paper, all of which were photocopies of old newspaper articles: two from October 1985, and one from February 1986. I spread them out in front of me. The first one was dated the 16th of October, and was a copy of the front page of *The Garshaigh Herald* – a paper I knew had stopped being published in the early 1990s. The article George had encircled was not the main piece, but was a shorter column near the bottom of the page. It read: 'Local Child Missing: Father Accused of Kidnapping'.

Written in a bombastic style by Edmund Stewart (a name I didn't recognise), it read as follows:

The venerable Father Senan Malone, Parish Priest of Garshaigh and its environs, has asked this newspaper to put out a call to all her loyal readers. Father Malone has been consoling a local mother, whom he says is 'bereft'. The good woman, Ms Winifred Tobin, of the Dunshire Road, reported to him that the father of her child, from whom she is estranged, has abducted their son and taken him to Australia. Father Malone told your correspondent: 'Obviously I am concerned that this little boy may be in the hands of a parent whose morals have been compromised. I do not know which parish he resides in in Australia, and although I do have a name, I have been unable to locate him through the usual channels. I know that many of your readers will know the gentleman to whom I am referring, so I am putting out a request to anyone reading this who might be aware of the whereabouts of this gentleman to pass the information on to me at the parochial house, so I can set the boy's mother's mind at ease.' Ms Tobin was unavailable for comment.

The second piece, a short column, was taken from page two of the paper and was dated a week later. The headline read: 'Woman at Centre of Abduction Dies Tragically'.

The local woman whose child was kidnapped by her husband and taken overseas, possibly to Australia, has died suddenly under tragic circumstances. She has been named by the gardaí as Winifred Tobin, of Dunshire Road, Garshaigh. Ms Tobin has been living at that location, it seems, for the past fifteen years, but her movements before then are not known, and local authorities are anxious to locate family members so her affairs can be settled. All information to the garda station in the town.

The final copy was from page thirty of the paper. It was simply headed: 'Hoax'.

The story covered in this publication last October, relating to a child that had been allegedly taken, against the will of its mother, by his father to Australia, has proven to be a cruel hoax. Winifred Tobin, who died in tragic circumstances, had raised the issue of the child's absence with our esteemed parish priest, Father Malone, who did his best to trace the boy, whom Ms Tobin named as Thomas, after his estranged father. Following her death, Father Malone and the local gardaí doubled their efforts, and a call for information was sent out through all local media, including your trusted weekly paper, The Garshaigh Herald. *It seems, however, that all these attempts to bring the lad back to his home place were misplaced. Investigations have unearthed no records of Ms Tobin ever having given birth to a child in any of the nearby hospitals. Father Malone was told that the boy, who was reported to be about ten years old, had been baptised in Ennis, but there is no evidence to support that claim either. Her nearest neighbours live two miles from her, and they admitted they had never seen the boy, and he was*

not enrolled in any local schools. When Ms Tobin's house was
visited by gardaí following her death, they found only a child's
bike and a home computer with some games, but no children's
clothes and no other evidence a child had ever been in the house.
It seems likely that the poor woman was beset by some kind of
delusion, in which, possibly through loneliness, she imagined a
child. In truth, Ms Tobin was rarely seen about the town of Gar-
shaigh and, living rurally, had little contact with others. 'It seems
we failed this woman,' Father Malone told the paper when we
spoke to him over the weekend. 'If someone had reached out to
her, perhaps things would not have ended so badly.'

A photograph accompanied the piece. It was of the living room
of Winifred Tobin's house. Although very grainy and in black
and white, I could make out an old-fashioned tube television, a
low coffee table in front of it. Sitting on the table was the home
computer mentioned in the article. It was a ZX Spectrum.

George Taylor was waiting for me when I got to Stanbridge's later
that evening.

'Thanks for digging out those pieces, George,' I said when I was
seated. 'It must have taken some time.'

'You know I'm a history buff. Your bringing up the story made
me curious. I used my usual research techniques, so going back
through the local papers was the first thing I did. The myth I told
you previously is, I believe, the local population's attempt to process
the events in the story you saw in those news clippings. They say
small towns have long memories, but in fact, I think they have a

remarkable capacity to twist facts to suit the cultural mores of the time.'

'How do you mean?'

'You saw that Father Malone, the priest hereabouts back then, chastised people for not having reached out to the poor woman in the middle of all of this. A rebuke from a man of the cloth in 1986 would have been taken very seriously, and I believe he backed it up by berating his congregation from the altar, too. He told them that a needy person had been in their midst and they had turned their backs on her – where were the Good Samaritans in Garshaigh when this lonely woman was, for want of a better term, going mad?'

'So, out of shame, they changed the story?'

'You know better than I do how folk memory works. The details of the story changed a little at a time, over a period of years: the events were adjusted so that, in the new version, they happened in secret. That way, no one could have helped, so the guilt was removed. The child became real – if you're going to have a horror story, you might as well make it as awful as possible. Incest was thrown in for good measure, the great taboo. The tale became ghoulish for Halloween nights. Not real. Therefore nothing to be ashamed of.'

'Not real? Isn't there a chance there was a child, though?'

'Why do you think so?'

'Just because there's no record doesn't mean it didn't happen. I've encountered kids before who were home births, never saw public health nurses, didn't attend school – it's not usual, but it does happen. And George, there are details of the story that Gregory couldn't have known. His friend is called Thomas. And the computer in the photo is the one he says his night visitor talks about ... there's something going on here, and I'm damned if I know what it is.'

George Taylor had a sip of his ale and thought for a moment.

'Digging into this further offers us some problems,' he said. 'Almost no one in Garshaigh knew Winifred Tobin. Father Malone spoke to her when she came to him about her son going missing, but I don't think he had much of an idea of who she really was or what she was like. Her neighbours would have known her a little, although even that knowledge was sketchy, from what I can gather.'

'Are any of these people still living locally?' I asked.

'Yes. Father Malone is in a nursing home, but still lucid, I believe. And some of the neighbours are still hereabouts, if you'd like to call on them.'

'Where did she live?'

'Well, the answer to that will tickle you, I'd say.'

'Why?'

George smiled, but the expression did not have a lot of humour in it.

'Winifred Tobin's house was about two and a half miles away from where the Finnegans live. Had they lived there at the time, they would have been one of Winifred's closest neighbours.'

29

The next day I rang the nursing home where Father Senan Malone was currently residing, but was told by one of the staff that he would be staying with a niece in Galway for a few days. I was tempted to ask for a phone number, but decided to hold off. There was a strong possibility the old priest would have little or no memory of events that had taken place thirty years ago, anyway.

A phone call to Orla Finnegan informed me that she had done as I suggested and screwed the window latch shut. There had been no disturbances in the intervening couple of days, so I hoped this simple solution had solved our problem – if there really was one, and we were not just dealing with overactive imaginations; I was starting to feel we were all buying into the child's fantasy. I promised Orla I would call out to see her in a day or two, and headed into the newspaper offices to get some work done.

Robert Chaplin, my editor, was perched at his desk when I arrived, clattering away doggedly on one of the paper's hopelessly out-of-date computers. He acknowledged my presence with a grunt and a nod, never breaking the rhythm of his typing for even a second. I sat down at my own workstation and began to leaf through the pile of papers listing the items I would be covering in the next edition. It was the usual assortment of local stories, mostly involving community events and human interest (that week I would be interviewing a Garshaigh resident who planned to climb Mount Kilimanjaro to raise money for cystic fibrosis). I reorganised the pile in order of the work required by each piece, then set about writing the three that simply required reporting the information I had been given and therefore involving no research – things like flagging up a bake sale at the local pre-school.

Chaplin and I worked on in silence for an hour, until my companion got up to go outside for a cigarette.

'Robert?'

'What?'

'You're from Garshaigh originally, aren't you?'

'You know I am.'

Chaplin was a tall, skeletally thin man in his mid-fifties. He had dark hair shot through with grey, always looked like he needed a shave, and dressed in well-worn pinstripe suits.

'Were you working here in the mid-eighties?'

'I finished college in '85, worked for a couple of years in Dublin for the *Irish Press*, then came back here to found *The Western News* in '88.'

'So you never worked for *The Herald*?'

'No. I put it out of business by running a better rag. Your man who edited that sheet, Ed Stewart, he wrote like he was trapped in the 1950s. It was ridiculous. You tend towards the overblown and dramatic, but this guy was on another level entirely.'

'Any recollection of a story they ran in '85, '86. A woman called Winifred Tobin reported her child missing, then died all of a sudden. The paper reported that it turned out to be a hoax, there never was a kid to begin with.'

'Yeah, I heard about it. A lot of rumour and speculation involved, if I remember rightly.'

'Like what?'

'Can I go out and have my smoke?'

'I'll go down with you. I could do with some second-hand carcinogens, anyway.'

I got us both a styrofoam cup of coffee from the newsagent's across the street.

'This woman, Winnie Tobin, was an odd sort, from what I was told,' Chaplin said, resting his back against the wall. His eyes followed people as they came and went on the footpath opposite us. 'I didn't cover the story, but I did come back to Garshaigh most weekends, so I remember it fairly well. It caused a stir for a while until the next scandal blew up.'

He pulled on the cigarette and blew smoke out threw his nose.

'Winnie wasn't from around here, and no one seems to know where she came from or what drew her to Garshaigh. She lived out on the old Dunshire Road, almost in the woods. The only reason people knew she was around at all was because she had to come into town now and again to get supplies, but even that was irregular 'cause she bought in bulk. Had a standing order with the grocers, mostly tins and dried food, which was delivered to the house every couple of weeks.'

'What age was she?'

'No idea. Young enough that her having a kid was believable.'

'Any photos?'

'No. I saw her once or twice. She was a small woman, jet black hair, very pale skin. She looked like someone with a disability or a mental illness, you know, shuffling walk, head always bent, never made eye contact, muttered when she spoke at all.'

'What was the reaction locally when she announced her child had been abducted?'

'I think people were sympathetic. Why would anyone have doubted her?'

'Father Malone seems to have done his best for her.'

'He was very progressive. I mean, you have to realise, even though it was never mentioned or really talked about, this was a child born out of wedlock – illegitimate, as they said back then. By rights, Winifred should have been ostracised completely. Instead, Father Malone seems to have felt badly for her, and because of him she was supported by the community. For a while, anyway.'

'How'd she die?'

'How do you think?'

'Well, looking at the language our friend Edmund Stewart used, I'm guessing it was suicide.'

'Hanged herself from a tree in the woods.'

'Did she leave a note?'

'She didn't have to. The rumour mill was in full swing by then.'

'Tell me about these rumours.'

'Initially, as I've said, people just took her at face value. She'd fallen pregnant to this guy she called ...'

'Thomas.'

'That's it. She says he wasn't local, that they had met in Limerick or somewhere, fallen for each other and he'd followed her back to Garshaigh where they had a torrid affair, resulting in this kid. Passion like that, however, burns hot and fast, and they had a blazing row one night after which he stormed out and disappeared for ten years. So, she raised the kid by herself in the little house in the trees and they didn't hear from yer man at all, not so much as a letter.'

'It's not that weird, really,' I said. 'Fathers had less of a role in those days. And if they weren't married …'

'Quite. But once something makes its way into the media, and becomes a *cause célèbre*, well, she was actually asking people to talk about it, wasn't she? The first thing that came to light was that this lad, Thomas, didn't go to school. In 1985 this was almost unheard of. Add to that the fact that Winifred had no photographs of him.'

'Holes started to appear in her story.'

'It wasn't that she had no up-to-date snaps. She had no photographs *at all*. Not even baby photos. Once the talking began, it didn't stop. One or two people initially said they thought they'd seen Winifred walking with a child in the woods, but only ever from a distance, and no one could give a description or be quite certain. Those people started to question what they'd seen, and before long, it became clear that no one had ever met this kid – it was like he didn't exist. And, of course, no one had met the mysterious father.'

Robert paused to light another cigarette. He offered me the pack, but I shook my head. It wasn't that I didn't want one. I just knew one wouldn't be enough.

'I think she understood it was only a matter of time before she was caught in the lie. Garshaigh had taken her to its bosom for a moment, only to toss her aside. She was going to be humiliated, shown up as a fantasist. In her loneliness and craziness, I suppose it was more than she could handle.'

'So she took herself into the woods and ended it,' I said.

'Yeah. But it *didn't* end there. The talk went on. Some old biddy who lived a few miles down the road from Winnie started saying there *had* been a kid, that she had been a visitor at their house, and had tea with them. She *swore* to it.'

'She waited until the poor woman was dead to weigh in?'

'Indeed.'

'Convenient. So maybe Thomas Junior *did* end up in Australia, then.'

'This particular local gossip suggested that an excavation of the local woodland would prove that not to be so.'

'She said Winifred killed him?'

'Went mad and murdered the child. Just like in the old song.'

'*There was an old woman and she lived in the woods,*' I sang.

'*Weila, weila, walia,*' Robert finished.

'This wasn't taken seriously, though,' I said.

'Well, no one dug up the woodland floor, if that's what you mean,' Robert said. 'To be honest, it would be a massive job. Such a large area, and all the trees and roots and whatnot. I think the cops did have a look for disturbed ground, but gave up pretty quickly.'

'But the idea persisted.'

'Good stories always do. A few people started saying that this man, Thomas, was actually her brother or her father, and that was why the child vanished and why she topped herself. The boy was a deformed monster, so they hid him from everyone, and eventually took him away to a home, or suffocated him in his sleep, to put him out of his misery. That version got legs, let me tell you.'

'And what do you think?'

Robert took a final drag of his cigarette and flicked it away.

'I think a sad woman spent too long on her own and invented a reason to make people care about her. When she found out those people were, in actuality, pretty horrible, she decided to put herself somewhere they couldn't hurt her. It's as old a story as any of the others and just as tragic in its own way.'

'Maybe more so,' I said.

'Come on,' Chaplin said, patting me on the shoulder. 'The paper won't write itself.'

We went back upstairs and, despite everything, I managed to forget about the sad, strange tale and lose myself in my work for a time.

30

The next day I called out to the Finnegans, as promised. Orla met me with a smile, and we sat and chatted for a while. It was clear that the fear she had felt the night she called me to listen to her recording was all but a dim memory, and she seemed more relaxed.

'I asked Gregory about Thomas just this morning,' she said. 'He didn't seem all that interested in discussing him. Maybe it's over.'

'It's a little soon to be celebrating, but for what it's worth, I agree with you that Thomas is losing some of his attraction. Kids often grow out of these things.'

'I hope so. I'm not going to lie to you, it's been casting a shadow over everything these past weeks. Did you ever have the feeling you're being watched everywhere you go?'

I nodded. I had long learned that being quiet was sometimes the best thing I could do.

'Well, that's how it's been. I've started to hate the trees. It's like there's something hiding behind every one of them. Living where we do, that can be a real problem.'

'Hopefully we can put it all behind us very soon. Where is Gregory, anyway?'

'He's out back.'

'I'll pop out and see him before I go, if that's okay.'

'Of course. And Shane?'

I paused, my hand on the back door handle.

'Yes, Orla?'

'Thanks.'

I grinned and went on out.

Gregory was just beyond the fence, kneeling on the ground. He had his back to me and didn't look up as I approached.

'How you doing, Champ?' I asked, stepping over the iron fence and walking across the soft, yielding earth to the boy.

'I'm okay,' he said.

I sat down next to him. He didn't have any toys and was staring into space, his hands resting on his knees.

'Your mum tells me things have been good lately.'

'Well, they're not. Thomas is mad at me.'

'Why?'

'I tole him I can't go out at night no more.'

'Yeah. I can see why that would bother him. Can't he come and play with you during the day like most kids do?'

'He don' like the day so much. He says it makes him feel funny to be out in the day.'

'So he won't come and visit you anymore?'

'I din' say that. He was just here.'

'Was he? Where's he gone?'

'He runned off when he heard you comin''

'Is he still around? Can you call him back?'

Gregory shook his head.

'He scared of grown-ups. Says they mean.'

'I'm not mean.'

I was casting my eyes about the area as we spoke. I could see that there was a spot right in front of the boy that was squashed and flattened, as if someone had been sitting there for a time. I absently laid my hand on it, thinking I might feel the warmth of a body, but it was cold to the touch.

'I tole him that. He says you just bein' nice now, but you'll turn nasty soon enough.'

I shrugged.

'Well, you tell your friend that if he wants to come and play some afternoon, I'll bring ice-cream and any game for the Spectrum he chooses. You can get them for free online now, so he can have whatever he likes.'

'I'll tell him, but I don' think it'll do much good. He gets real scared sometimes.'

I sighed, and shifted so my back was against a tree.

'You know, Greg, I used to work with kids who were frightened of things – it's what I did for a really long time. I kind of still do, in a different way, at the school. If Thomas could tell me what's wrong with him – or if he wants to tell you, and then you pass it on to me – maybe I could help. It can't hurt to try, can it?'

Gregory thought about this, his face taking on a serious caste.

'I'll talk to him 'bout it when I sees him next.'

'Good,' I said, pulling myself upright. 'I'm going to head back to the house, say goodbye to your mum. You staying out here for a bit?'

He nodded and I started to walk back to the cottage. I had gone a few steps when he called after me.

'I axed him that thing you said 'fore.'

'What thing?'

'You said to axe him what was number one in the charts.'

I paused, suddenly remembering.

'What'd he say?'

'"Power o' Love" by Jennifer Brush.'

I laughed. 'You mean Jennifer *Rush*.'

'It a song,' Gregory said. 'He tole me it was the song people like best.'

'It's a song people liked best a long time ago,' I said.

'That's what he said, anyways.'

I made my farewells and drove back to the newspaper offices. Checking online I found that the power ballad in question had reached the number one spot on the 12th of October, 1985, in the UK singles charts, which was the one I assumed most children would have been aware of through the good offices of the TV show *Top of the Pops*, required viewing in most homes during that decade. The song had remained at the top of the hit parade until the 16th of November, when it had been unseated by Feargal Sharkey's blue-eyed soul version of 'A Good Heart'. It had been, without question, the biggest-selling single of that year.

I pulled out the articles George Taylor had copied for me, and checked the dates. Thomas had been reported missing by his mother on the 16th of October 1985, right in the middle of Jennifer Rush's dominance of the world of popular music.

If Gregory was making this all up, he was putting an awful lot of research into his fantasy. And I didn't think the Finnegans even had Wi-Fi.

DR B: What did you think was going on?

SD: I had worked with a family in the area before who had chosen to live as if it were still the early nineteenth century – no electricity, no running water, no TV, no internet, growing and foraging for their own food. It seemed reasonable to me that I might be dealing with a kid who was growing up in a house where mum and dad were stuck in the eighties.

DR B: But the similarities to the story in the newspapers …

SD: Some stories are archetypal – they seem to resonate and echo, and events repeat themselves. I didn't want to get bogged down in all of that. At this stage I had two little boys who had somehow found one another, and I was very concerned that one was being neglected, or was even living rough.

DR B: But you liked the mystery element of it. You were hooked.

SD: I was fascinated to see how it turned out, yes. The Finnegans are a lovely family – the two kids are sweethearts, and Orla has done a tremendous job raising them by herself. But a lot of what I do involves feeling your way – you find something to grasp on to, and then you follow that thread and you see where it leads.

DR B: And you like that journey, don't you?

SD: It's what keeps me doing this strange thing I do, yes. You never know what each day will bring.

31

I sought Maura out the following Monday, when we returned to school. Knowing she was habitually early, I arrived just as George Taylor was unlocking the gates at half past seven. When Maura got in at ten to eight, I was in the staff room already, sitting on the old couch just inside the door. She did not look happy to see me.

'You don't have to talk to me, Maura. I just want you to listen to me for a moment.'

She walked over to the mail slots and checked hers, which was empty, then went to the sink and put water in the kettle.

'I don't think you have anything to say I want to hear,' she said when it was plugged in and boiling.

'I was talking to an old friend of Tim's the other day.'

'You're not going to use Tim to manipulate me into talking to you,' she said through clenched teeth.

'If you want me to stop looking into Tim's death, I'll happily walk away from it. I only kept at it because I'd promised you I would.'

She snorted and sat down opposite me.

'It doesn't make much difference now, anyway, does it? He's dead. I messed up, just like I always do.'

'I think we both know you didn't mess up with Tim. From what I've been learning, he was a much more complex character than most people realised.'

She gave me a hard look, and then, as if the weight of the world was on her shoulders, put her head in her hands.

'Just leave me alone, Shane. You've done enough damage already. Can't you butt out of my life?'

'I'm your friend, Maura. That means I'm not going to turn my back on you when you're so clearly in pain.'

She looked up at me with a tear-stained face.

'It was all going so well. Then I asked him to come to that bloody party, and it all changed.'

'Changed how?'

'Nothing major – we haven't fought or anything like that – it's just like he's become colder towards me. More distant.'

I immediately felt myself bristle.

'And this is because of me? Has he said anything about me?' I asked.

'No. Not once. I asked about how you know him, don't think I didn't, but he said you weren't worth talking about.'

'He hasn't hurt you physically?'

'For God's sake, Shane, will you give it a rest!' she snapped. 'Rex is not violent, he never has been! He's obviously getting bored with me, that's all, and I don't think the welcome he got from you that night helped things one bit. You lived up to every fear he had about coming out of prison.'

I struggled to find the right thing to say. Gifford had very artfully twisted things so I looked like the villain, and I was forced to back-pedal desperately to get out of it.

'You know, we didn't talk that night, he and I. He knew I was going to be there and he wanted me to see you both together but he didn't approach me and not one word passed between us.'

'You didn't have to say anything – you *radiated* animosity.'

'If things have cooled off a bit, it has nothing to do with anything I said or did – it's all part of this game he's playing. Get away now before he does something really awful.'

She stood up sharply and walked to the door.

'You're an asshole, Shane. Keep away from me and keep away from Rex.'

She slammed out, leaving me alone in the staff room.

'But will Rex leave me alone?' I asked of the empty space.

I thought it unlikely that he would.

32

For the rest of the week Maura passed me in the corridors without acknowledging my existence, sat (on one occasion right beside me) in the staff room as if I was not there, and on Wednesday afternoon dropped a child to my classroom, managing to not even look in my direction. It was frustrating and upsetting.

On Fridays I usually worked at the paper, so it was purely by chance that I happened to pop into the school to pick up a book I had left in the drawer of my desk.

The building was almost deserted when I arrived, since it was after five o'clock. I knew George Taylor rarely left before six, however, so I was confident I would find the door closed but unlocked, and could whisk in and out without any difficulties.

I walked briskly down the dark hallway that led to my room, snapping the light on as I went in. The book, an old collection of nursery rhymes I had inherited from my mother and which I used when working with children who suffered from speech disorders, was just where I'd left it, and, placing it in my shoulder bag, I headed back out the way I'd come.

As I crossed the yard, I spotted Maura at her car and decided on the spur of the moment to make one last attempt at reconciliation – we were about to embark upon the weekend, and I felt lousy leaving things to fester as they were.

'Maura, can I just have a quick word, please?' I asked, trotting over.

At the sound of my voice, she rapidly scooted inside the vehicle, closing the door with a sharp bang. I got to the Fiesta just as she was starting the ignition, and bent down to the window, which was partly open.

'Come on, Maura. Let's not leave things like this, eh? You don't have to hang out with me anymore, but can we at least be civil to one another?'

As I peered through the window at her, I realised she was trying desperately to turn her face away from mine. Suspicious, I moved around to the front of the car so I could look directly through the windscreen. What I saw filled me with rage: my friend's left eye was puffy and bruised, her lower lip split and scabbed over. The injuries looked fresh – by Monday, when I was supposed to have seen them, they would have been blackened and even more dramatic. Maura put her foot on the accelerator and revved, but I laid both my hands on the bonnet of her car and stood firm.

'Maura, if our friendship still means anything at all, please talk to me.'

As I watched, I saw all the fight going out of her. She visibly sagged and, removing her hands from the wheel, gave me a simple nod. I opened the passenger side door and slid in beside her. She said nothing at all for a long while, simply staring ahead, her arms folded across her chest. I watched her from the corner of my eye, not wanting to force things.

'I made him do it,' she said at last.

'How?'

'I made him angry with me.'

'I thought it was me he was angry with.'

She started to laugh, but then thought better of it because of her injured lip.

'I wanted us to get that closeness back, that we used to have in the beginning. I shouldn't have nagged him. He needed me to be more understanding.'

'Listen to yourself, Maura. You're defending the man who hit you. Imagine if one of your students told you a boyfriend had hit them? What would you say?'

'It's complicated. He's … he's hurting. His time in prison made him harder than he really is.'

I turned so I was facing her fully.

'Do you remember the night of the party? When Gifford arrived, what did I tell you?'

'If you are truly my friend, Shane, you won't play the "I told you so" card. Please be kinder to me than that.'

'I'm not gloating, I promise you. Just want you to think back. What did I tell you that night?'

'You said he was dangerous.'

'What else?'

'You said he was a predator. That he preyed on women.'

'I also told you he was brilliant. He is a chameleon, changing to suit whatever he thinks people expect. That's how he managed to win you over – he became what you wanted him to be.'

Maura shook her head.

'I have to believe he is more than that.'

'He *is* more than that. There are myriad aspects to his character, but none of them are good.'

'What does that say about me?'

'It doesn't say anything about you. This is about him, Maura. He wants you to think you have a part in it.'

'So I am just a helpless victim.'

'No. You're not helpless. You can help yourself, and a lot of other people, too.'

'How?'

'Come with me to the police and have him arrested. He's on parole. He'll be back inside before the night is out.'

She laughed again, but this time as a kind of throaty sound inside her so she didn't have to move her damaged mouth.

'I can't do that.'

'Why not?'

'Because he's all I've got.'

'Not true. You have me. You have George. You have all your students. You have a good life, Maura. Gifford has you believing you are empty and useless and dependent. Don't give in to him.'

In a lunge she reached over me and flung open the door.

'Get out.'

'I'm not leaving. Not like this.'

She grabbed my arm with a fierce grip.

'If you care for me at all, even a little bit, be on your way and never mention this conversation again.'

'But Maura ...'

'Go, please!'

I heard the urgency. There was no mistaking it.

'I'm going.'

'Thank you.'

I got out of the car and watched her drive away. I felt as if I had been the one Gifford had struck. And I knew that was what he wanted.

33

The next day when I went out to my car to drive to the farmers' market for my weekly shop, the vehicle wouldn't start. In fact, the engine wouldn't even turn over. I had never had so much as a moment's hassle with the Skoda, but having owned a classic car for many years I was well used to mechanical hiccoughs, and simply called the garage.

An hour later I was gazing into the bowels of the engine with Mark, a long-haired and bearded mechanic.

'Well, you see what the problem is,' he said.

'No.'

'Really? It's pretty obvious.'

'Mark, I called you because, while I love cars for their aesthetic qualities and their convenience, I know virtually nothing about fixing them.'

'You don't see something missing?'

I looked again, and then even I saw what he was talking about. 'I don't fucking believe it.'

'Yup. Someone has taken your battery.'

I shook my head in disbelief.

'Can you get me another one?'

'It'll set you back around sixty euro. I'll have to order it in.'

'How long?'

'It's Saturday, dude. It's gonna be Wednesday of next week at the earliest.'

Cursing, I slammed the bonnet down.

'Gerry Blaney might rent you a runaround for a couple of days, if you're stuck.'

I nodded and swore again. As if Gifford wasn't enough, now I was going to have to do business with another snake.

I put Millie on her leash and we walked the mile or so to the car showroom the aforementioned Gerry Blaney ran just outside the town. The man in question was a tiny (barely five feet and two inches in lifts) but charismatic member of a prominent local family, with whom I had had some dealings when I first came to Garshaigh. These interactions involved him manipulating a case I was involved in from both sides, and ended with his brother being placed in long-term psychiatric care, and his nieces, nephews and sister-in-law all ending up in sheltered accommodation. Somehow, while all this was going on, he managed to broker a deal over the family land that resulted in several million euro finding its way into his pocket. Gerry also found the time to send thugs after me in an attempt to persuade me to sway the opinions of social services, first one way and then, for no reason I could ever discern, the direct opposite way. To rub salt in the wound, on one occasion during all this, he had me beaten up. I didn't like the little man, and believed him to be utterly mercenary and self-serving, but his was the only car rental business in town, so my options were somewhat limited.

I explained what I wanted to the girl behind the counter and five minutes later Gerry Blaney was leading me to a corner of his car lot, talking in his booming baritone about the relative merits of this model over that one. Despite the fact that I had met him quite often, the man's appearance always amazed me. He was about fifty-five years of age, and on this occasion he wore a suit that managed to be decades out of fashion (wide shoulders, glaringly shiny, loud, patterned material) while still looking as if it cost him more money than I was likely to see in a year. His skin was a deep, walnut brown, suggesting it came from a bottle or the rays of an oft-used sunbed, and his hair had been sprayed and coiffured so it stood in an artificially dyed wave several inches above his head, in a failed effort to make him look taller.

Yet there was nothing funny about him. He was as supremely confident as only a man who knows he is the ultimate alpha male in his territory can be: Gerry Blaney was the richest man in Garshaigh, and he was very happy with that fact.

'Here is my recommendation,' he said, stopping at a 2004 model Volkswagen Golf. 'It's a nippy little car, and I can give it to you at a very nice rate, in light of our close friendship.'

'I'm not really fussy, Gerry,' I said. 'I only need it for a few days. And while I am flattered, I must admit to being unaware our relationship had progressed to the level of "close friendship".'

Blaney laughed raucously and thumped me (low) on the back.

'You're a tough cookie, aren't you, Dunphy? Let's have a drink and I'll fill out the paperwork.'

We sat in his office and he poured me a tumbler of scotch. It was too early for me to have a drink, but I cradled it in my hands and watched as he filled out the forms with a chunky, diamond-encrusted pen, which looked too big for his tiny, slender hands.

'So, the Skoda giving you trouble? I thought they ran like clockwork. German engineering and all that.'

'Oh, it's running fine. There has been foul play I'm afraid. Someone I annoyed a few years ago has returned to claim their pound of flesh.'

Blaney finished what he was doing with a flourish and pushed a page over for me to sign.

'You do have a habit of pissing people off, don't you?'

'What can I say? It's a talent.'

'If you need any help, you know where I am. There are some lines you don't cross, and messing with another man's vehicle is one of them, as far as I'm concerned.'

I pushed the page back and handed him his ridiculous pen.

'Well, it's good to know you *have* a line, Gerry. Here was me thinking you were completely without scruples.'

He tossed me the keys for the Golf.

'You wound me, Shane. And we such close friends.'

'You'll get over it.'

'Happy motoring. Remember what I said – I'm here to help should the need arise.'

'If things get that bad, I'll be in serious trouble,' I said, and left him to his mid-morning whiskey.

34

By the time I made it to the farmers' market all the good produce was gone. In an effort not to completely waste the day I drove over to the nursing home where Father Senan Malone lived. He had been due to return the previous day, so he would be well settled now and, I hoped, up for visitors.

St Hilda's was a privately run establishment based in a rambling converted manor house. The grounds were well kept and, inside, the building had a sense of light and happiness about it that gave the impression it was well run. The staff here took pride in what they did.

I had rung ahead, so Father Malone was expecting me. I found him sitting by the window in his large, airy room, dressed in an open-necked grey shirt and dark blue slacks. There were pictures of landscapes on the walls and a large, wooden crucifix hung above the door, the only religious artefact I could see. The elderly priest was a tall and regal man, despite the ninety years he told me he had lived as we sat down. He offered me tea and busied himself about the room getting biscuits and laying them out, then asked me if I minded him lighting his pipe.

'It's your home, Father,' I said. 'I am encroaching on your hospitality. Smoke if you feel like it.'

'In these days it is often seen as a rudeness, is it not?'

'I like the smell of pipe tobacco. Please, light up.'

He produced an ornate-looking meerschaum pipe from a drawer in the low table, and put a match to it, getting the bowl glowing as he liked, then sat back contentedly.

'Would you be so good as to pour the tea, and while you're at it, tell me why you're here on such a beautiful Saturday afternoon. I daresay you could be doing any number of more desirable things than sitting inside with an old fuddy-duddy like myself.'

I picked up the teapot, a fine bone china affair with forget-me-nots painted in a chain about the side.

'I'd be very grateful if you would talk to me about a rather tragic case you were involved in back in the 1980s.'

'You'll have to be more specific – as you are aware, those were tough times in Ireland. I met a lot of sad people.'

'Winifred Tobin.'

Malone sat back and drew deeply on the pipe, blue smoke coming from his nostrils in tendrils.

'Now that is a name I have not heard spoken in many years.'

'I hadn't even heard of her until a week ago.'

'And how did you come by her?'

'You probably wouldn't believe me if I told you.'

'I have nothing left but time, and I always enjoyed a good story.'

'I teach children with learning difficulties in St Smoling's, in Garshaigh,' I began, and with the old priest listening intently, I spent the next twenty minutes or so telling the story of Gregory Finnegan and his imaginary friend. I mentioned the links and similarities the events had with Winifred and her real or imagined son, and how the folk tale about the ghostly boy in the woods seemed to be somehow mixed up in it all as well. When I was done, he removed the pipe from his mouth and ran his fingers through his thin white hair.

'That is an odd tale to be sure,' he said.

'Is there anything you can tell me that might help?' I asked. 'I had hoped that Thomas might disappear as Gregory and I got closer and I got him to open up, but I have to tell you, he seems to be as entrenched as ever, and the details are shockingly real and vivid.'

'I don't know what I can say to you,' Malone said. 'It's almost thirty years since I encountered Winnie Tobin and her child. If he were real, and if he did survive, he would be about your age now, maybe a little older. You have mentioned child-sized footprints and voices that clearly don't belong to an adult. Could a grown man even fit through Gregory's window?'

'No,' I said. 'I don't believe so.'

'So are you genuinely suggesting this is a ghost, or a changeling, or something of that nature?'

'No, Father. I've been working on the idea that we could be dealing with a child who might in some way be connected with the Tobins. A kid so familiar with the events that destroyed Winifred that he has subsumed them and made them his story, too. A cousin, a grandchild maybe … what do you think?'

Father Malone nodded thoughtfully.

'That would of course be dependent on the premise that Winifred's child was real and survived.'

'Is that possible?'

The old man stood.

'Let's walk in the gardens. A conversation like this would be much more bearable out of doors, wouldn't you say?'

We strolled down a cobbled path that led around a wide pond and then into the edge of a wooded area.

'These are the same woodlands as the ones where Winifred lived,' Malone said to me. 'They stretch for miles. If you went into the trees just here and struck out east, you'd come to her old house, eventually.'

'They say you were closer to her than anyone,' I said. 'Did she make it all up?'

'I met that woman for the first time in 1984, just before Christmas,' the priest said. 'I hadn't even known there was a family living in that cottage on the Dunshire Road – I thought it was just a derelict shell. I happened to be going that way one evening to visit a sick parishioner when I saw a light on, so I decided to pay my respects. I found this half-starved looking, lank-haired, frightened little woman. That first visit I only stayed for about half an hour, but I got her to invite me back, and over a few weeks I became, perhaps not her friend, but at least a warm acquaintance.'

'So you would have known if she had a child.'

'Oh, she told me, on the very first night, that she did.'

I stopped dead in the middle of the narrow path. Shadow and light played over us both as the winter sun shone through the trees, making patterns on the stones and on our faces.

'Did you ever meet him?'

'Not as such, no.'

'So she made him up, then?'

'I would not be so quick to jump to that conclusion.'

'What?'

'The first evening I visited there was pop music playing loudly in one of the bedrooms. She explained this by telling me that her son, Thomas, was in there playing on his home computer. She always told me he loved that machine. She maintained she had trouble getting him off it, but she insisted he go and play outside at least once a day.'

'Yet you never saw him?'

'On several occasions Winifred and I would be sitting outside in her little garden, which she kept quite well. It was just a grove among the trees, an area with a bit of grass growing and she had a fallen log she used to sit on. She called it her bench. On more than one occasion she would gesture out into the forest and say: *'There's wee Thomas out for his walk.'* I'd look out in the direction she indicated, and as sure as I am standing here with you, I am almost positive I saw a boy. I even waved at him once, and I swear to you he waved back.'

'And it wasn't a trick of the light,' I asked, 'you're certain there was a child there?'

'No. You see, I'm *not* totally sure. Looking back, after all that has passed, I am now full of doubt. *She* was so certain, I just never questioned her. A child's bike, an old thing but well-maintained, was always in the hallway, and there was often fresh mud and leaves stuck to it, as if it had recently been taken out. And that computer was regularly plugged into the TV when I went in, with some queer game or other on the screen. She would always say she'd asked Thomas to go and do some study or to go out for air so the adults could talk. And she would say: '*There he is going past the window,*' and I'd look and maybe see a shadow or a fleeting movement, and that would, in my head, be him. This child.'

'But you never spoke to him?'

'Just before she told me he had been taken by his father I was on one of my visits – I was calling several times a week, by then – and as I was leaving she called in through the door of the room where she said Thomas was doing some homework, '*The Father is going home now, Tommy,*' and a voice called back, '*Goodbye, Father.*''

'A child's voice?'

'I thought so at the time.'

'Do you think his father really did come and take him, then?'

'I don't know, Shane. She said this man was a brute – violent, drunken, sexually depraved. She told me she had been scared for her life. That was why I made such an effort to have him found. I was terrified for the boy if he was with this monster.'

'Did you ever manage to trace the father?'

'Absolutely not. I have never found any evidence that he existed. But that does not mean he didn't. She may never have had his real name. With no details and nothing to go on but a first name and a loose description, it was next to impossible to make any headway looking for him.'

'She didn't even know his last name?'

'Thomas was all she could give me. She said he was tall and dark. Not handsome, but intense looking, with close-set brown eyes. She met him in a bar in Limerick, or so she said.'

'Did she often go to bars on her own?'

'Not when I knew her. But she told me she used to be quite …
um … wilful.'

'Were you surprised when she killed herself?'

'No. I had a terrible feeling it was coming. As people turned
against her, she became paranoid, erratic in her behaviour. I
talked to her about staying strong and riding out the rumour mill
that was destroying her. I still believed her completely then. I
was disgusted with the whole community when she took her life
– I didn't feel anyone had offered her the friendship or support
she needed. I fought to bury her on hallowed ground. When the
Bishop refused me, I went ahead and did it anyway.'

I smiled at that.

'Good for you, Father.'

We walked for a while, the light getting dimmer as the trees grew
thicker overhead and about us. Somewhere to our left I heard a
pheasant's staccato call.

'There was a suggestion she killed the boy,' I said.

'Yes.'

'Any thoughts on that?'

'What do you want me to say?'

'I don't want you to say anything. I mean, do you think she was
capable of doing that?'

'I think anyone is capable of doing almost anything.'

I could sense the conversation was coming to its close.

'Will we go back?' Father Malone asked.

'Let's,' I said.

He turned as we reached the door of his room. It was clear I
wasn't going to be invited in this time. I thought I'd save him the
embarrassment of dismissing me.

'Well, I'll leave you, Father. Thanks for your time.'

'I'm sorry I couldn't be of more help,' he said. 'But there really isn't anything to be gained by dredging up such an unpleasant episode from the past. I'm quite worn out just talking about it.'

'No problem. But Father, before I head on, could you just answer me one more question?'

He sighed, but forced a smile and looked at me expectantly.

'Certainly. What is it?'

'For better or worse, putting everything else aside, just giving your personal opinion and nothing else, would you say that Thomas Tobin really existed, or was he an invention of a mentally ill woman?'

Father Malone opened the door to his room and stepped inside. He looked back at me.

'I don't know, Shane,' he said, a thread of annoyance coming into his voice. 'I've told you all I can. I'd like to rest now, if you don't mind.'

And he closed the door and left me standing in the hallway alone.

I went out to where I had parked the Golf. A driveway wound in and out of the trees for a quarter mile before meeting the main road, and as I drove it my mind was still on the conversation I'd had with the priest.

I wasn't sure I had really learned anything. In fact, I reckoned I might be even more confused than before. It was a feeling I was getting increasingly used to. I rolled down the window to let some air in. To my left, the trees cleared for a moment, creating a small patch of earth skirting the driveway on which a few scraps of grass grew. There, standing in the middle of this negative space, looking completely out of place, was a small boy. He was wearing an anorak that looked to be light brown in colour, with a large hood. His blue jeans were scuffed and dirty, and he had dark hair cut in an old-fashioned, long mop-top style. His eyes seemed impossibly large and dark, and they followed me as I drove past.

I slammed on the brakes and was out of the car and running back the way I had come almost before the Volkswagen stopped. I thundered into the clearing, but there was no one there. I stood where the boy had been, listening to the wind in the trees and the purr of a rock dove in the boughs above me. Had I seen a boy? Was he there at all, or was I starting to go a little crazy myself with all this strangeness?

I had no idea, but *was* sure I was being watched as I got back into the car. The feeling continued until I left the trees behind and got on the main road for home.

DR B: Did you really see a boy, or do you think your mind was playing tricks?

SD: If you had asked me that an hour after the fact, I would have told you beyond any doubt that I saw him.

DR B: And now?

SD: I don't know. I remember him so vividly, right down to the fact that one shoelace was undone. But then, you tell someone they are sleeping in a room where a ghost has appeared, and you tell them what other people in that room have experienced and before too long, they'll swear blind that they experienced those things too. I've studied psychology. I know how suggestible people can be.

DR B: Why do you think I was suggesting it was a ghost that you saw? You told me you saw a little boy. There are lots of little boys, and the most obvious explanation is that you simply saw a child who happened to be playing in those trees because he lived nearby.

SD: Right. That is the most sensible explanation.

DR B: Or do you think it might have been something else?

SD: For instance?

DR B: Well, do you think it might have been this boy, Thomas,
        who, it seems from your story, might or might not be
        the ghost of a child who might or might not have been
        murdered thirty years ago?

SD: Sounds crazy, doesn't it?

DR B: Crazy is my business, Shane.

35

The phone rang as I was preparing dinner later that evening.

I held it between my chin and shoulder as I chopped some bulb fennel. It was Devereux.

'Are you still following up on the death of young Tim Fox?'

I paused before answering, because I actually didn't know whether I was or not. Maura didn't seem to care one way or the other, caught up as she was in the turmoil Rex Gifford was putting her through. The kid was dead – why spend any more time on him? *Maybe that's what everyone said while he was alive,* a voice intoned somewhere at the back of my mind. *If even one person had made more of an effort, perhaps he would still be alive.*

'Yeah, I suppose I am,' I said at last. 'What have you got for me?'

'Do you remember a gentleman by the delightful name of Ballsack who was Tim's chief tormentor on The Shaker?'

'The name does ring a bell, yes.'

'He's just been released.'

'And?'

'He's been set up with a job waiting tables at a greasy spoon in Blackalley. I thought we might join him for breakfast tomorrow, seeing as he's in my backyard, so to speak.'

'You think he'll even give us the time of day?'

'You'd be amazed at how ready ex-cons are to talk about their time on the inside. He'll play hard to get at first, but he'll open up soon enough.'

'Really?'

'Take my word for it.'

'Well, so far I've only heard from people who were, more or less, on Tim's side. This'll certainly be a new perspective.'

'I also seem to recall us wondering if Ballsack might have taken advantage of Tim's isolation in those final days – he was without protection while Stills was in solitary and would have been ripe for the picking.'

'It can't hurt. Can you text me the address?'

'Don't you have a pen and paper?'

'I just thought—'

'I do not *text*, Shane. Write this down.'

He gave me the address and I scribbled it on the back of a receipt.

'Be there at nine tomorrow and we'll see what we can learn.'

He hung up and I went back to cutting my veg.

'What do you think of that, Millie?' I asked the dog. 'Breakfast served by a rapist. I get to meet the nicest people.'

Millie did not even open one eye, so I decided to keep any future thoughts on the subject to myself.

36

Ballsack proved to be as terrifying as his name suggested: six foot four inches in height, with a shaved head half-covered in a Celtic tattoo tapestry; he was so muscular his upper torso looked almost deformed. He waited tables at The Checker Grill, a truck stop and diner situated amid the housing estates and flat complexes of Blackalley. Devereux and I had the good sense to order before letting the object of our visit know who we were or why we were there.

'It is never a good idea to upset someone handling your food,' my companion pointed out as we looked over the menus.

The fare was surprisingly good and the coffee excellent. It was ten thirty by the time the crowd started to thin out, and by then I had drunk enough of it to feel as if electricity was charging through my veins.

'I thought you were cutting back,' Devereux said as I beat a staccato rhythm on the table top with my fingers.

'Looks like I fell off the wagon, doesn't it?'

Ballsack (a badge pinned to his tee-shirt said his real name was Brian) strode down the aisle and began to wipe down the table opposite ours, where a family had just finished their meal.

'Might we have a word?' Devereux asked.

'You want more coffee?' the tattooed man asked, looking disbelievingly at me.

'No, thank you. It's something of a private matter, so you may want to wait until your break so we can discuss it quietly.'

'You from probation?'

Brian/Ballsack had a strangely high-pitched voice, which made me think his vast bulk may have been augmented by the use of steroids.

'No. This is a personal matter,' I said. 'Nothing you say will be passed on to the authorities.'

'If it's personal, then I don't have to tell you fuckers shit.'

He turned and began to walk back towards the kitchen area.

'We could just ask you about Tim Fox right here, among your colleagues and the patrons of this establishment,' Devereux said.

He did not speak loudly, but his voice carried remarkably well. Ballsack stopped, turned and moved briskly back to where we sat.

'I don't know what you heard, but it is a fucking lie!'

'We just want to hear your side of it,' I said.

'When is your break?' Devereux asked.

'Eleven.'

'We'll be right here. Come down and join us when you're ready.'

At the top of the hour Ballsack slid into the booth beside me. I am not small, but I felt utterly dwarfed beside him.

'I'm trying to go straight,' he hissed at Devereux. 'I don't fuckin' need you comin' round tryin' to stir up shite when I'm workin', do you fuckin' get me?'

'Timothy Fox,' Devereux said calmly.

I often noticed that when I was with my friend around a certain type of person, the conversation seemed to happen around me, as if I was not really very important. It's not that I was being ignored, it was more that a language was being spoken that I could converse in on a basic level, but in which Devereux was fluent.

'What do you want to know about that loser?' Ballsack said.

'I heard he was a favourite of yours.'

'What the fuck is that supposed to mean?'

'You tell me.'

'I'm not a faggot, if that's what you're gettin' at.'

'No. You are an opportunist.'

'Sorry?'

'You take your pleasures where you can. Who the owner of your orifice of choice might be, and whether or not they consent to your ministrations, is of little concern to you.'

Ballsack began to turn a bright shade of puce. He was not used to being spoken to in this way, and he looked ready to blow.

'I'm givin' you and your pal here twenty seconds to get the fuck out of my restaurant,' he said, in a voice that was shaking with fury. 'If you're not out by then, I'm gonna—'

I didn't see Devereux move. He appeared to remain exactly where he was sitting, but suddenly Ballsack was sprawled against me, clutching his throat and gasping for breath.

'Relax for a moment while you get your breath back,' Devereux said, leaning in close. 'I just punched you in the windpipe, which causes your breath to be cut off for a little bit. It'll contract in a second, so don't panic.'

He placed what looked like a soothing hand on the bigger man's shoulder, but I could see he was actually holding him upright. Ballsack finally sucked in a shuddering breath, and the colour began to return to his face.

'There you go,' Devereux said, patting his arm gently. 'Now, are we okay to continue our conversation?'

The giant beside me nodded, still grasping his throat.

'You and some of your associates raped and tortured a young man named Tim Fox while you were on The Shaker. I believe a friend of mine, Monty Drew, and later an old enforcer called Bob Stills warned you to keep away from him. I know Stills ended up in the hole for a time, and I want you to tell me, truthfully, if you molested Tim in any way that might have caused him to take his own life.'

Ballsack tried to speak and only a croak came out. Devereux stood up and fetched a fresh glass, pouring the man some water from the jug on our table.

'Thanks,' he said, once he had swallowed some.

'Don't mention it.'

'Look, man, I'll admit I took advantage of the lad. I probably went a bit rough on him, but when Drew told me to back off, I fuckin' backed off, alright? I didn't want no trouble from that big fucker.'

'Drew was released, though,' I said. 'So you didn't need to worry about him anymore.'

Ballsack looked down at me, and then at Devereux.

'You I know,' he said. 'Everyone around here knows you. You are entitled to respect because of what you done in the past.'

He looked at me again as if I was something he had just stepped in. 'But who the fuck is this?'

'He is a trusted friend of mine,' Devereux said. 'If you extend respect to me, he should be the recipient of the same courtesy. Conversely, if you insult him, which you are coming perilously close to doing, then you cause an affront to me.'

Ballsack sniffed and drank some more water.

'Drew went home. Sure. Did I fuck around with the kid when he left? Yeah. A little bit. He needed to be taught some manners.'

'What about Bob Stills?'

'He was not as … um … as dedicated to looking after the lad as Drew had been. Ah, he warned me to back off, but he didn't keep a very close eye, and I scared the little bollix enough so he wouldn't tell on me. Said I'd hurt him real bad if he did, y'know what I'm sayin'?'

I could feel myself getting angry. 'No, *Brian*. I don't know what you're saying. Why did you feel the need to sodomise and orally rape this kid to "teach him manners"?'

'He was full of himself,' Ballsack scoffed. 'He was a real mouthy little fucker. If I didn't keep him in line, he was gonna get himself killed.'

'And a simple conversation wouldn't do that?'

'You don't really know how it works inside, do ya, Slick?'

'Apparently not,' I said. 'But it seems from what you're saying that human debasement is the usual medium of communication.'

'So Stills did not protect Tim at all?' Devereux asked, quieting me with a glance.

'Ah, eventually he found out what I'd been doin' and had a word with me, like.'

'Bob Stills had a word with you?'

'He warned me to leave the lad alone.'

'Did he warn you with his fists?'

The big man pulled the neck of his tee-shirt down a couple of inches to reveal a livid scar.

'He used his fists and a razor blade,' he said. 'He made his point.'

I shuddered. 'And you left him alone after that?'

'I'd have been fuckin' crazy not to.'

'That doesn't really answer the question,' I said.

'After Bob Stills, that sick, twisted little psycho, had his chat with me, I never went near Timmy Fox again. I kept me distance, alright?'

'Was he involved with anyone else on The Shaker?' Devereux asked.

'How d'ya mean "involved"?'

'Did he have any other friends? Did he run with a gang? Was he working with anyone?'

Ballsack stroked his shaven head as he thought.

'I have a feelin' he useta do some runnin' for Wheeler Bowyers.'

'And how was he paid for those services?'

'I don't fuckin' know. What am I, his fuckin' accountant?'

'Did you ever work for Wheeler?'

'Yeah, once, when I got on The Shaker first.'

'And how were you paid?'

'In product. Most people want their wages that way, y'know?'

'Just to be clear, we're talking about drugs, aren't we?' I interjected.

'Yes, Shane,' Devereux said. 'Heroin is the product we are discussing. Were there any other payment options available?'

'Some want protection. Others want cash put aside for when they get out.'

'Did you ever have the impression that Tim was under Wheeler's protection?'

'No. And your boy din't ever strike me as the kind of guy who wanted a nest egg for when he was released, either.'

'No?'

'Naw. He wasn't that smart. He wanted to make life easier for himself on an immediate, day-by-day basis, y'know what I'm sayin'?'

'Alright,' Devereux said. 'I'll know where to find you if we have any more questions.'

Ballsack muttered something inscrutable and went back to the kitchen.

'Help me to process all that,' I said when we were alone again.

'As we suspected, Bob Stills did not do a very good job as Tim's protector, and Ballsack did indeed return to harassing him. Someone told Stills, though, and he put it right. The biggest thing we learned was that Tim was working for a very dangerous man, probably the most powerful individual behind bars in Ireland at the present time.'

'This Wheeler guy?'

'Wheeler Bowyers, yes. His involvement adds a whole new aspect to things.'

'How so?'

'Shane, where there is a mysterious death, where there is any degree of chaos and unhappiness, where there are people suffering – where you encounter those things and Wheeler Bowyers is in the near vicinity, you can be absolutely certain he is the primary cause.'

'How could Tim have been involved with this guy and Drew and Bob Stills not know?'

'I would guess that Drew knew and did not want to mention Wheeler out of fear – he didn't want to draw any negative attention on to him in case word got back he had been the one who pointed the finger. Stills' reasons are probably more complicated: Wheeler might have paid him off; Stills might be working for him now and doesn't want to rock the boat; Stills might simply not have wanted to tell us out of spite. He and I have a muddled history.'

'What do we do now we have the information?'

Devereux took out a plain leather wallet and dropped some notes on the table.

'Follow the trail of destruction.'

'You are talking figuratively again.'

'We haven't a hope in hell of talking to Wheeler – he knows me and hates me, and that means he probably knows you, too.'

'I'm flattered.'

'We have other options, though. Bowyers may be incarcerated, but he still runs all his enterprises on the outside from his cell on Salt Island. He has a vast network of suppliers, dealers, prostitutes, pimps and moneylenders at his beck and call, and he knows down to the smallest detail what all of them are doing. He has always been a micro-manager, but that style of coordination has its challenges when you don't have ready access to the people involved.'

'And?'

'And that means Bowyers needs someone to do that face-to-face business for him. His Commander on the outside is an old friend, a man called Goitre MacDonald. I'd be very interested in knowing more about the merchandise that was going into The Shaker during

Tim's tenure there. We've been told some of it was bad – poison, effectively. Goitre would know down to the last grain what was in each specific mix that was shipped out of Bowyers' factories. He would know because Wheeler would want to know, and Goitre is Wheeler's eyes, ears and brain on this side of the fence.'

'I don't see how that helps. Tim died of an overdose, and Bernie told me that he thinks he took some bad drugs by accident.'

'That doesn't wash. If this stuff was bad, Wheeler and his people would have been fully aware. Most stuff that goes into prisons is of terrible quality anyway – why send in high-end product when you have a captive population, most of whom don't care what they're taking as long as it gives them some kind of a buzz? I don't believe Wheeler Bowyers would have let something into his territory that was going to cause deaths. Why draw that level of heat down on himself? There's still a piece of the picture missing. We should talk to Goitre.'

'And you and he are friends?'

'We have a cordial relationship.'

'Do you know where we might find him on a Sunday morning?'

'As it so happens, I do. He walks his dogs in the People's Park every Sunday. If we hurry, we should be able to keep him company on his ramble.'

'I could use a walk to work off all this caffeine,' I said.

'Then we shall kill two birds with one stone,' Devereux said.

We didn't leave a tip.

37

We drove across the city in Devereux's black Volvo. He operated the vehicle like he did everything else: as if he had been built to do it – it was like the car was an extension of his nervous system.

'Karl, why are we still doing this?'

'Doing what?'

'Working this case?'

Devereux threw me a quick glance.

'I'm doing it because you asked me for help, and because Tim Fox is like a thousand others I've come across. He deserves to have someone go that extra mile, even if it means we're just trying to find out what happened to him. I think that means something.'

'I dunno, Karl. He wasn't the saint everyone made him out to be. He dealt drugs. He was violent. He used the label of intellectual disability as a shield so he could behave like a thug and commit crimes.'

'No one's perfect.'

'Fuck it, Karl, this was someone who probably *should* have been in prison. From what I've been told he squirmed his way out of it a dozen times before they caught him on the parking fines. What Ballsack did to him was absolutely appalling, and I know he died, and that's terrible and shouldn't have happened, but in a lot of ways this was something that was going to catch up with him sooner or later anyway. If the drugs didn't kill him, he'd start a fight with someone a lot bigger and tougher than he was and end up dead. I mean, he brought it all on himself, really.'

'If I turned up murdered one morning, would you say the same about me? God knows I have done enough in my life to warrant it.'

'You've gone out of your way to make amends for everything you did.'

'And are you the one to decide when the balance is in my favour? I did very, very bad things. I hurt people, some of whom did not deserve it. Can you really say I have set that right?'

'You made the decision to change.'

'I was a lot older than Tim Fox when I had my road to Damascus moment. Who knows what he might have become given the chance.'

'What I'm saying is that we are putting a lot of time and energy into this, and there's no way it will make any difference. Tim is gone and he's not coming back.'

'When I was still involved in the life, I knew a kid called Aleck,' Devereux said. 'He was typical of the kind of youngsters we had coming up through the gangs back then – he came from a family that didn't care a jot whether he lived or died, and school had not even tried to engage with him. He was angry at the world, angry at himself, prepared to do anything to prove he had the kind of ferocity that would mark him out for success in our business.'

'Sounds a lot like how you described your younger self to me, once.'

'If anything, I was worse. But yes, you get the picture. Aleck did all the usual jobs we got kids to do: he ran errands, cleaned up, helped with mundane tasks like cutting product, and eventually he graduated on to more, shall we say, hand-on tasks.'

'By which you mean committing acts of violence on behalf of his employers.'

'Precisely. He turned out to be very good at it. I always thought it was because he was so full of rage that he had almost no sense of fear, or of self-preservation. His physical safety was secondary to getting the job done.'

'Sounds borderline psychotic.'

'Perhaps. I heard a story once, from a mutual friend. He and Aleck had been sent to destroy a meth factory run by a rival organisation, but they were ambushed before they completed the task. Aleck was already known, by then, as an up-and-coming member of our syndicate, so they weren't going to kill him outright. The two lads were taken to a warehouse outside the city and tortured, beaten pretty solidly for two days. Well, my friend said that after five hours of abuse, he was prepared to tell them whatever they wanted, and did: he gave names, what business transactions were going down, when and where deals were to be brokered; whatever he knew, he spilled it. Aleck was more senior, and they knew he had a lot more information, and they told him they were not going to stop until they were sure he had spilled everything. They broke his fingers one at a time, they burned him with cigarettes and lighters, they cut him with carpet knives until there was not a bit of him that wasn't a wound.'

'Jesus, Karl,' I said.

'My friend told me that Aleck never answered a single question. He laughed at them, he screamed, he cursed and threatened to kill them and their families. They took turns beating him until their fists hurt, then they used baseball bats and hurleys. They attached him to a car battery and shocked him. Still nothing.'

I shook my head. 'You admire him.'

'You listen to this and all you see is a thug who got his just deserts. To me, Aleck was someone who found a code of honour he was prepared to live and die by. Surely that is to be admired.'

'What you have just described to me seems like needless suffering. The people he was protecting weren't worth it.'

'They were to him. The gang had become his family, for better or worse. He was protecting the people who meant most to him.'

'Would they have done the same for him?'

'I don't know,' Devereux said. 'Maybe, maybe not. When they realised they had got everything they could from my friend, they put him into the boot of a car and dumped him on some waste ground in Blackalley. He was so far down the pecking order he was not even worth killing, and they wanted someone to pass on that Aleck was alive and couldn't hold out much longer. His body was found three weeks later. He had to be identified by his dental records. I won't go into any more details about what was done to him before he died, suffice it to say he had a horrific end. But I *will* tell you this – for a long time, it was just accepted that he must have broken, and any operations he knew about were moved, and all plans were changed. People were watching, expecting a war. It never happened.'

'Aleck held out,' I said.

'It seems he did. Despite unimaginable torment, he never gave in. He allowed them to torture him to death, and died without so much as a whisper.'

We had reached the gates of the park by then, and Devereux found a parking space a few yards up the street.

'Aleck was filled with so much pain and anger that at times he seemed almost feral,' Devereux said as we walked towards our meeting with the man called Goitre. 'But there was something decent under all that fury, something that, despite the worst degradation and abuse I have ever seen inflicted on a human being, kept him from betraying the people he cared about. I'm not saying he could have been "saved" or "put on the right track"' – Devereux said these last words while making inverted commas in the air – 'but I am saying that Aleck, and people like him, should never be written off as human garbage.'

We reached the gates and paused.

'There endeth the lesson.'

In the park people were sitting on benches drinking coffee out of cardboard cups. A woman in brightly coloured spandex jogged past, listening to music through earphones. In the distance, I could see a slim man walking two tiny dogs. Even though I was still preoccupied with Karl's story, I wondered if that was our man.

'Karl?'

'Yes?'

'A friend didn't tell you that story, did he? It was you who was in the warehouse with Aleck. You were put in that boot and allowed to live.'

'How did you know?'

'Instinct, I suppose. I don't know what to say. I'm … I'm sorry you had to go through that.'

'That's not the point I was trying to make. I want you to see that, just because Tim Fox isn't the vanilla character we were led to believe, he is still a person as deserving of our intercession as anyone. Let's see it through to the end, for better or worse.'

'Okay,' I said. 'Let's follow the trail and see where it goes.'

If I had known where it was leading, I would have walked away then and there. Instead, I went to meet a gangster.

38

Goitre MacDonald was a stringy beanstalk of a man who looked to be at least a hundred years old. I assumed his unusual moniker came from the fact that he appeared to have no neck, his head melding with the rest of his body, making him look as if a giant boot had come out of the sky, Monty Python-style, and tried to squash him. He was wearing a long overcoat and a wide flat cap, which actually served to accentuate his odd appearance.

'I don't like being interrupted while I am walking the girls,' he said. 'This had better be extremely fucking important.'

'There is a rumour circulating that you shipped bad medicine onto The Shaker,' Devereux said. 'A young man died, an employee of Mr Bowyers, as it happens.'

'People die. What has that to do with me?'

'They say your drugs killed him.'

It looked as if Goitre was walking two emaciated guinea pigs, but going on the information that they were, in fact, dogs, it appeared 'the girls' were some kind of Chihuahua. Millie could have eaten them both in one mouthful.

'If you ingest enough paracetamol, the kind you can walk into any supermarket and buy right off the shelf, it'll kill you. I still don't see how this concerns me.'

'You know precisely what is in each shipment, because you oversee all the cutting of raw product. I just want to know if the kid we're looking into died because he didn't realise it was dangerous and took too much. Did you give him a killer drug, Goitre?'

The old man sat on a bench and took the rats off their leads. They scampered onto the grass and started sniffing here and there, just like real dogs.

'You don't need me to tell you the shipments we send to The Shaker are always piss-poor. Prisoners will take what they can get and be fucking thankful for it.'

'Of course.'

'But one thing I do not want to do is put a killer drug where my boss is – you don't shit where you sleep, right? I don't know what kid you're talkin' about, but I can assure you that every single consignment of H that I signed off on was heavily diluted with cornflour, and therefore was *less* fuckin' lethal than the shit you'll buy on the street. Now, if he wanted to use it to kill himself, your guy could have taken a bucketful of it and got the job done, but he'd've had to *plan* to do that.'

'The young man I'm referring to was called Tim Fox,' Devereux said.

One of the hamsters ran behind a patch of weeds and all but

disappeared. Goitre whistled and it re-emerged, wagging its scraggy tail.

'Yeah, I know the name. Don't think I ever met the kid. Wheeler seemed to like him, though. Said he was a crazy little bastard. He family to you or somethin'?'

'Something. Did he work for Mr Bowyers during his entire sentence?'

'No. Wheeler reached out to him. Bob Stills asked for him to be taken on as a favour, if I remember correctly. I think the kid had been drawing some negative attention from some sex fiends, you know how it is inside. Fuckin' degenerates. Stills thought this kid having an association with Wheeler would look good for him. You run with someone like Wheeler, the butt munchers leave you alone.'

'Do you have any recollection of the circumstances surrounding his death? Anything that might help us get a clearer sense of what happened?'

'Not really. I know Wheeler was annoyed over it, but other than that … *meh*.' He shrugged in an exaggerated manner.

'Why was he angry?'

'Like I told you, he liked the lad, and he seemed to feel there was some kind of interference in it all. I don't know if the young fella had been moonlighting with a minor competitor, or if one of the sodomites had been sniffing around again. I think Stills looked into it some.'

'If you remember anything else, please would you get in contact with me?'

Goitre made a clicking sound with his tongue, and his two gerbils scuttled across the lawn towards him.

'I owe you something from who you were before, Devereux. You went away for a stretch, and you never turned over on any of us. I appreciate that.'

'Your boss doesn't.'

'You were an independent operator, and Wheeler never liked it. He prefers to have exclusive rights to goods and services. You wouldn't be bought.'

Devereux smiled darkly. 'I still won't.'

'So I hear. Now, would you two kindly fuck off and leave me and the girls to our walk? I'll ask around and see what comes out of the undergrowth. It's probably not gonna be much, though. People die. On The Shaker, people usually die unpleasantly. It's a fuckin' fact of fuckin' life.'

He put the leads back on his chinchillas and, nodding at Devereux and then at me, walked slowly on down the path.

'Nice man,' I said.

'Among his kind, he is not the worst,' Devereux said.

It was two in the afternoon as I hit the road for Garshaigh. The phone call that set all hell loose came at three.

39

I was considering pulling into a motorway rest stop for a sandwich when my phone began ringing. I didn't know the number.

'Hello?'

'Can I speak to Shane Dunphy, please?' It was a female voice.

'Speaking.'

'My name is Helena, and I'm ringing you from St Swithin's Hospital. Maura Bellamy has just been admitted, and she asked me to call you.'

I gripped the wheel involuntarily. 'What happened?'

'She says she was attacked by an intruder. She's pretty badly bruised and ... well, could you come over? She needs to have someone with her, and she says she doesn't have a close relationship with her family.'

'I can be there in forty-five minutes.'

Helena, a slim, dark-haired nurse, who looked to be about twelve years old, showed me to Maura's bed at the end of a ward. Curtains had been drawn around her to give a false sense of privacy.

'She's been beaten pretty badly,' the girl told me. 'You should prepare yourself.'

'Was she ... I mean, was it just *physical* ... I mean to say ...'

'She was also sexually assaulted,' Helena said, and put her hand on my arm. 'I'm sorry.'

I clenched my eyes shut, but angry tears seeped out anyway.

'Can I get you some tea or anything?'

I shook my head and gathered myself as best I could. 'I'd like to see her now, please.'

Maura was asleep when I went behind the curtain. Her face was a mess of cuts and bruises, her left arm bandaged heavily and her right covered in a plaster-of-Paris cast. I sat in the chair beside her bed and cried. This was on me, and there was no denying it.

She woke with a start two hours later. I gently shushed and soothed her, and she settled back onto the pillows.

'Shane, you came,' she said through her ruined mouth – I saw that her front teeth were broken. 'Would you mind calling George for me? I don't think I'll be able to make it back to work on Monday.'

'Already done. He asked me to give you his best.'

'Thanks, Shane.'

I took one of her hands in both of mine.

'Maura, I would like your permission to speak to the police. He has to be stopped now, don't you see?'

'I can't do that,' she said gently. 'People can't know what happened to me.'

'He'll keep doing this to people, Maura. He's not a person like you or me. He doesn't understand things like we do, and the pain he has caused you is absolutely meaningless to him. He won't ever feel any remorse. He has to be stopped, don't you see?'

It took her some time to respond – she seemed to drift a bit, and I wondered if she was falling back to sleep. Then her left eye opened slowly and focused on me; her right one was swollen closed.

'You were right about Rex. Why did you have to be right?'

'I'm so sorry, Maura. If there is anything I can do …'

'I don't have very much, Shane. I haven't talked to my family in years. I've got a little bit of dignity. Don't let him take that away from me, along with everything else. Garshaigh is so small half the town already knows I'm in hospital. I can cope with them thinking I was attacked in a robbery. I don't want them to know the truth. Please, Shane.'

I squeezed her hand gently. 'Okay.'

'He asked me to tell you something.'

I froze. 'What did he say?' I whispered.

She took a deep breath and then tried to wet her shredded lips with a dry tongue. I held a glass of water to her lips, and she drank a little.

'What did he say, Maura?'

'He says it's your move.'

And I lost all sense of reason for a time.

DR B: You seem very upset.

SD: You could say that.

DR B: Stay with it. Let's see where it leads us.

SD: My friend was raped and beaten to a pulp by a man who was really only interested in hurting me. In effect, the violence Maura experienced was a message Rex Gifford wanted to send.

DR B: A message he wanted to send to you. You feel that this whole thing is really just an extended conversation between you and this man Gifford. A dance, almost.

SD: I wouldn't use that image, but yes.

DR B: Have you any idea how narcissistic that sounds?

SD: I beg your pardon?

DR B: What age is Maura Bellamy?

SD: I dunno – forty, forty-five, something like that.

DR B: And you told her, in no uncertain terms, that Rex Gifford, this man she was in a relationship with, was a convicted sex offender, and a violent one at that.

SD: You know I did.

DR B: And do you not feel that, armed with that knowledge, Maura was fully able – and entitled – to make up her own mind about whether or not she wanted to continue her dalliance with him?

SD: Dalliance?

DR B: You speak about her as if she is ten years old. This is an educated woman. It is, of course, devastating what happened to her, and you should be upset, but please stop taking on the blame for everything that happens to those around you. There is one person to blame for this, and we know who that is.

SD: It still wouldn't have happened if he wasn't coming after me.

DR B: Has it occurred to you at all that your determination to believe that what happened to Maura is really all about you might actually in some way belittle what she went through?

SD: What?

DR B: Maura was raped. She was beaten and belittled and traumatised. Yet you turn the whole thing around and make it about yourself. Isn't that hugely insulting and demeaning to your friend?

SD: I never thought about it that way.

DR B: Think about it now. Take yourself out of the equation. Forget your feud with Gifford and your history and all of that, and just focus on Maura and her pain.

(*There is a pause and some shuffling.*)

DR B: Do you need to take a break?

SD: (*Slightly muffled.*) She didn't fucking deserve it, okay? I know it's … it's not all about me, but I didn't know what else to do. (*Takes a shuddering breath.*) She was my friend and I let her down. Sometimes I feel it's all I ever do, is let people down.

DR B: And do you feel that people let you down too?

SD: I don't know. Sometimes. Maybe. But that's not the fucking point, is it? I try to fix things and all I end up doing is hurting people. Again and again.

DR B: Who do you turn to when you need help? Who looks after you? Sometimes the strongest thing we can do is realise we can't do it all by ourselves.

SD: (*Mutters something unintelligible.*)

DR B: What was that?

SD: (*Still muttering.*) I said that I don't know how to do that.

DR B: Maybe that's something we can work on together.

SD: Maybe.

40

I am not proud of what I did next. I can only offer in my defence that I was not thinking straight.

Maura teetered back into a troubled sleep, and I sat for another hour beside her bed, a feeling of utter hopelessness enveloping me. I knew I had to do something, but Gifford had me backed into a corner. My first instinct was to call Devereux. He was a man who was used to dealing with unpleasant people, and would probably not find Gifford much of a challenge. Devereux tended to elicit fear in most people, and I thought he might be able to impress on Gifford the need to disappear and never cross my path again.

I was already demanding a lot of my friend, however, and did not want to prevail upon him again. Devereux had rarely asked me for favours in return, and sometimes I felt as if our relationship was a one-way street, with me permanently the one on the take.

I was fully aware that the right thing to do was go directly to the police. A serious crime had been committed, and there was no doubt whatsoever in my mind that a DNA test would show unequivocally that Maura's attacker and Rex Gifford were one and the same. That would result in him being returned to prison post-haste for many years to come.

But of course Maura would have to give permission for such a test to be carried out, and she was not going to do that. In reality, the police were no help at all.

That left me with one course of action.

Gerry Blaney lived in a sprawling mansion on the outskirts of the town. Just like the man himself, the overall layout and décor of his home skirted the bounds of good taste – there were twin brass lions perched atop the gate columns, and a statue of Elvis Presley in all his Vegas glory adorned a fountain in the middle of the front lawn.

The door was opened by the blonde girl who worked as Blaney's receptionist. Instead of the tight-fitting business suit she wore to work, this evening she was dressed in a bright pink tracksuit.

'I'm sorry to disturb you so late,' I said, 'but could I please see Gerry?'

'Mr Blaney is having his massage, Sir,' Blondie said with a smile. 'Could you make an appointment for the morning?'

'Could you tell him it's Shane Dunphy and I need his help? I wouldn't be here if it wasn't an emergency.'

She considered me for a moment, then stepped aside. 'Wait in the lounge, please.'

I sat in a room that managed to blend leopard print and gold lamé in creative ways. Over the fireplace there was a picture of Neil

Diamond in his iconic 'reach for the stars' pose from the 1980s remake of the film *The Jazz Singer*.

After what felt like forever, Gerry Blaney arrived, dressed in a white terry cloth bathrobe. 'Shane. A drink?'

I accepted the whiskey.

'How can I be of service?'

He sat in an armchair opposite me.

'I have a problem, and I think you might be the only person who can help me with it.'

'Does this problem have anything to do with the interference your vehicle experienced recently?'

'As it happens, it does.'

He sipped his drink and smiled. 'Here's how this works. All I want is a name, a description and where the problem might be found. I do not want to be told anything else. Are we clear?'

'Yes.'

'How vigorously do you require this matter to be dealt with?'

'As firmly as you can without resorting to violence.'

'That might not be possible. Most problems, in my experience, require a little rough-housing.'

'I want him to leave and not ever return here. I want him scared good and proper. But do it without hurting him. Please.'

Blaney sighed and leaned forward. 'You're upset. Whatever has happened since we last talked, it seems to me that it's pretty serious. Your response needs to be equally resolute, or this fucker will just continue to walk all over you.'

I drained the scotch in one gulp. He stood and got the decanter and refilled my glass.

'No offence intended, but coming to you is bad enough,' I said.

'I think he wants me to come down to his level. I can't do that, or he's won.'

Gerry nodded. 'Gimme the details. I'll get back to you in a day or two.'

'Thanks, Gerry.'

'After this,' the little man said as he wrote down Gifford's name and possible location, 'we're quits, you 'n' me.'

'I never thought we weren't,' I said wearily.

'You know what I'm talkin' about – that business last year with my nieces and nephews and the old place and all.'

'Yesterday's news, Gerry,' I said, standing up. 'I'm not holding any grudges over that.'

'Maybe not, but we're still quits, right?'

'If you say so.'

I walked out without saying goodbye, praying I hadn't just opened Pandora's box.

41

I spent most of the following days with Maura, when I didn't have to work. The staff in the hospital were wonderful and I could sense my friend slowly making her way back from the abyss. We spent the time chatting about mundane things. I brought in gossip magazines for her to read and DVDs for us to watch on her laptop.

Helena told me the doctor had tried to get Maura to see a psychotherapist, but she refused outright.

'She says she's had enough of people poking around in her head, whatever that means,' the nurse told me ruefully.

It was the fourth night of her stay. We had just watched a movie called *Enough Said*, a smart romantic comedy starring James Gandolfini and Julia Louis-Dreyfus, which we both really enjoyed.

'You have sat through five chick flicks with me,' Maura said as the credits rolled. 'You can bring in some action movies if you like. I won't shrivel up and die.'

'I think I could use some gentleness for a little bit,' I said, smiling. 'And anyway, I like James Gandolfini.'

'Yes, I remember him from that TV show *The Sopranos*, and films like *True Romance*, both of which were pretty violent.'

'Did you like the movie, Maura?'

'Yes.'

'Then stop complaining!' I shut off the laptop, poured us both some water and ate a couple of grapes I had brought in but which Maura had barely touched.

'Have you seen him?' she asked suddenly.

'Who?'

I pretended to play dumb to give me some time to gather my thoughts.

'You know who.'

'I hoped you meant someone else. I have not seen Rex Gifford, no.'

'I bet you wanted to go looking for him.'

'I want to fucking kill him, Maura.'

'Thank you. Thank you for feeling that.'

'You're welcome.'

'I think he wants to kill me, Shane.'

'No, don't think that. He's mean and cruel and wicked, but, God help us, he's already done what he does.'

'He texted me this morning.'

I tried to keep the panic from my voice.

'Did he?'

'Want to see it?'

'I don't need to. What did he say?'

'It was just one line. He says he can't wait for me to get out of hospital.'

I closed my eyes. This was going from bad to worse.

'What do you want me to do?'

Tears began to run down her face.

'I don't want you to do anything, Shane. I think I'm going to have to call my dad.'

A wave of relief washed over me. 'Do you think you can? I didn't think you talked anymore.'

'He and I had a huge row ten years ago when I resigned from the private school where I worked. He set me up with the job, you see, but I wanted something more challenging. He was furious, told me not to bother him ever again if I left to work with "idiot children out in the sticks".'

'Time heals a lot,' I said. 'And he's your dad, at the end of the day. He wouldn't have wanted something like this to have happened to you.'

'I know. I just wish I'd picked up the phone to him months ago, before all this happened. I feel like such a failure.'

'You're not. You're one of the strongest people I know. Gifford tried to break you, and he couldn't do it. You were too strong for him.'

'I feel pretty broken!'

We sat together quietly.

'You need to be safe until we can do something about Gifford,' I said. 'I'm working on it, but it'll take a bit of time. You're not running away, you're just taking yourself out of the line of fire for a while.'

'I'll call Dad tomorrow. Tell him I want to come home.'

'I bet he'll be really glad to hear from you.'

He was, too.

42

I couldn't face going home to an empty house that evening, so I rang Orla Finnegan and asked if I could call out to see how things were going.

'I'd be happy to see you, Shane. I was going to call you anyway.'

'Everything alright?'

'Come ahead out and we'll talk.'

I stood in the doorway of Gregory's bedroom and looked at the board Orla had fixed over the broken windowpane.

'When did it happen?'

'Last night. I heard the smash from my room. When I got in here, Gregory was sitting bolt upright in bed, with glass all over the floor. This seems to have been what did it.'

She pointed to a rock, covered in lichen, which had been left on the floor by the window.

'Where was the rock when you came into the room?'

'About there.' She indicated a spot three feet from the doorway.

'Fuck it,' I said.

'What?'

'He couldn't have done it himself, could he?'

'No.'

'Did you see anything else?'

'It was all very frightening. Gregory was screaming, Aongus had woken too and was very upset. I called the police and they came out this morning, but all they could say was that it's probably some local kids making a nuisance of themselves.'

'Has he been talking about Thomas at all recently?'

'No. It had gone very quiet.'

I scratched my head and yawned.

'Here's what we're going to do,' I said.

Orla bundled the two boys into the back of her car and followed me back to town, where I picked up a heavy overcoat, a flask, a torch and Millie, and then got in her car and drove back out with them to the house.

'Are you sure you want to do this?' Orla asked after she had put the kids to bed.

'I think it's the only reasonable thing left *to* do,' I said. 'I don't swallow the idea of ghosts throwing rocks through windows. It's too adolescent. Someone is doing this, and it's time we sat them down and had a serious conversation.'

'Okay. Well, here's your tea – I filled your flask, no milk or sugar, just how you like it. I've made a couple of sandwiches as well. Come in if you get too cold; I'll leave the door open.'

'Don't. I'll be fine. I don't want any access points to the house available other than that window. We parked the car in the shade so I'll be completely in shadow, but with a good view of the side of the house Gregory's bedroom is on. If anyone tries to get in, I'll see them.'

'And if you do catch someone?'

'I shall shine a torch in their faces and effect a citizen's arrest. I also have the local garda station on speed dial, and a terrifying dog at my side.'

We both looked down at Millie, who was fast asleep (and snoring) on the kitchen mat.

'If you say so.'

It was eleven o'clock when Millie and I snuck out to the car. She curled up on the back seat and went straight back to sleep, and I sat in the front passenger side, poured myself some tea and waited. The minutes dragged by. A fox squealed and cackled far off in the woods, making Millie stir as something primordial in her recognised the call. I passed the time by making lists in my head: ten best books I had ever read; five finest meals I had ever eaten; twenty songs I really wanted to learn but hadn't got around to. I was tempted to turn on the radio, but didn't want to do anything that might warn our intruder of my presence. I sipped the tea sparingly, knowing from past experience that nothing botches a stakeout more definitively than having to step out from your cover to take a pee.

Despite my best efforts, at one thirty, I had to do just that, ducking behind a tree across the road.

I was returning to the car when two things happened simultaneously: Millie starting going berserk in the back of the car, yelping and whining dreadfully, and I spied a small figure moving slowly out of the trees beyond the Finnegans' house. I paused, blinking in the shadows, trying to be sure I was really seeing what I seemed to be seeing.

I was little more than twenty yards from my quarry, but I could not make out any features – all I saw was a small, person-shaped shadow that moved very smoothly, despite the rough ground it was traversing. Even though I knew there was a fence to scale, the intruder seemed to be on one side of it one moment, and the other the next without pausing. It reached the drainpipe, seemed to stop, as if checking to see if anyone was about, and then began to steadily rise up it, moving hand over hand with no apparent effort.

That was my cue. I broke cover and sprinted across the road, dragging the torch from my pocket and switching it on as I ran.

'Hey! Hey you!' I shouted.

I reached the side of the house and shone the beam of the light on the figure which was now at the broken window and saw, for a brief instant, a wide-eyed, pale face peering down at me from the folds of a hooded coat. I had a moment of recognition; it was the boy I had seen in the clearing at the nursing home. Then he was gone.

One moment he was there, the next simply ... not.

I stood in the dark, blinking stupidly, gripping the cold base of the drainpipe as if it might somehow hold the answer. I paced up and down, shining the torch here and there, hoping to spot him making good his escape. I saw nothing.

Millie had calmed down, so I let her out, and then using a key Orla had given me, I let myself into the house and went into Gregory's room (he was sleeping with his mother that night). The board was still firmly in place and had not been tampered with at all.

The child hadn't got inside. So where had he gone?

DR B: He just vanished?

SD: He was there and then he wasn't. It wasn't like he faded or went transparent – there was just no one at the top of the drainpipe anymore.

DR B: You had been under tremendous pressure, Shane. You were tired and stressed.

SD: And it was dark. I know all that.

DR B: Are you sure it really was a child? Could it have been an animal – a large cat or one of those … what do they call them, pine martens? They're quite big and you were in the woods.

SD: I thought I saw a boy. That's all I can say.

DR B: Could it be that someone had a grudge to bear against Orla Finnegan? Another interpretation of what could have been going on is that she was the victim of a cruel joke … had you considered that Rex Gifford might have been behind this too?

SD: It's not his style. If Gifford was involved, Orla would have turned up raped and beaten. He'd have gotten his feet under the kitchen table and then done something awful.

No, Rex had nothing to do with it. This was something else entirely.

DR B: But what?

SD: Damned if I know.

43

'You actually saw him?' Orla asked the next morning.

'Yes. I think I've run into him before and he vanished that time too. Quick-footed little bugger.'

'Who do you think he is?'

'I don't know. I have a feeling he's connected with a family who lived in this area thirty years ago. Does the name "Tobin" mean anything to you?'

'No.'

'Mmm. Well, keep the boys with you until we can get that window fixed, and I'll see if I can't track down this kid now we know for definite he is out there, and seemingly unsupervised – attentive parents don't usually let their children roam the countryside on their own at half past one in the morning.'

'There's a group of Travellers camped up the road a stretch,' Orla said. 'Maybe he's one of them.'

'When did they arrive?'

'About a fortnight ago.'

'The timing is wrong then, but it can't hurt to check them out.'

The Travellers (sometimes – incorrectly – referred to as gypsies or tinkers) are a nomadic, tribal people indigenous to Ireland, closely linked to the Romany people. The particular group Orla was referring to had set up camp in the woods about five miles from the Finnegan homestead. I could see their collection of vehicles through the trees and parked just beyond them. The space they occupied could hardly even be called a clearing – they had navigated between some widely spaced thickets, a small fire, surrounded by blackened stones, smouldering at the centre of it all.

They had three old mobile homes, three saloon cars to tow them and a red Hiace van. They watched my approach with unguarded suspicion. I counted fourteen children of varying ages as I walked the short distance from where I had parked. Four older women and some teenage girls stood at the doors of the caravans. They looked tired and frightened. I saw no men.

'I wonder if you can help me,' I said, trying to get a good look at each child to see if any of them resembled the one I had encountered the previous night.

'What d'ya want?' a swarthy, heavy set woman asked.

'I'm not trying to move you on,' I said. 'A friend of mine lives a few miles up the road and she's been having some trouble with damage being done to her house – now it's been happening long before you arrived, so I am not suggesting you have anything to do with it. I just wondered if you'd seen anything.'

'Seen anythin' like what?' a girl with straight black hair and feline green eyes asked.

'I don't know – anything out of the ordinary.'

'We don't see nothing, only what we wants to see,' one of the older women said. She was dressed in a worn woollen cardigan and a tweed skirt, her long hair greasy and tied back in a loose ponytail. 'We keeps ourselves to ourselves.'

'These disturbances are happening late at night. Have you heard any strange sounds? Anyone moving about in the woods?'

'We don't go into the woods at night,' a boy of about twelve (with a shock of red hair) piped up.

'I don't blame you,' I said. 'It can be quite dangerous.'

'We can't help you, Sir,' the first woman cut in. 'I'm sorry for your friend's troubles, but we do not want any hassle. You can tell her we will be moving on later today, so she need have no concerns about us.'

'Why are you moving on?'

'This is a bad place.'

'Is it?'

'Goodbye, Sir, and good luck to you.'

With the vaguest movement of her head, the woman signalled to the group and everyone disappeared into the caravans, leaving me standing alone.

Almost.

When I got back to my car, the red-headed boy had beaten me to it, and was peering in through the back window at Millie. I had left her on the back seat with a rug thrown over her – Travellers are well known for their love of hare coursing and dog-fighting, both of which pursuits involve greyhounds, and I am always wary they might be tempted to liberate her for their own uses.

'Is that your greyhound, Mister?'

'It is, and she is not for sale, and I do not race her, and I do not take her coursing,' I said, pre-empting the frequently asked questions I tend to get about my dog.

'What's her name?'

'Millie.'

'Can I pet her?'

I looked at him warily. 'I'll take her out for a moment, but that's all, okay? I have stuff to do, and I'm already late.'

I opened the door and Millie surged out, then suddenly cringed down on the ground, looking about her with great discomfort. This display of emotion was not like her, and I was shocked by it.

'What's wrong, girl?' I asked.

'Our dogs don't like it here either,' the red-haired boy said, stroking Millie gently. 'My ma says it's 'cause this is a bad place. A *dark* place. We're moving as soon as me da and me uncles get back. They have some tradin' to do in town, but when they gets done with it, we're goin'.'

'And why is it such a terrible spot?' I asked. 'What's wrong with the place?'

He looked around him, as if checking to see no one else was listening. 'I'm not meant to tell. Me gran says you country people wouldn't understand.'

'Country people' is the term Travellers use for any person (whether they are rurally based or not) who lives a settled, non-nomadic lifestyle.

'Try me,' I said. 'I've never seen Millie act like this. What's going on?'

'If I tells ya, ya can't let me ma or gran know I did, okay? They always says we has to keep settled folk like you ignorant.'

'It'll just be between you and me.'

'Alright then.' He looked quickly about again to be sure the coast was clear. Then in a whisper: '*It's cause of the ghost.*'

I felt cold fingers run down my spine. 'A *real* ghost? In the woods?'

He nodded, his eyes wide, his expression solemn.

'What kind of a ghost?'

'A boy. He lives around here, I think. You see him through the trees. Sometimes he comes so close to our camp, I think he's gonna walk right in and sit down next to us.'

'Have you seen him?'

He nodded. 'We all seen him. My ma said he was just curious about us and he'd go away when he saw we was good people, but he keeps comin' back. My gran did prayers and stuff to banish him, but they din't work.'

'What does he look like?'

'Just like a boy.'

'How do you know he's a ghost and not just some kid, then?'

'I thought he *was* a kid first time I seen him. It was one evenin' last week, after we'd had dinner. I was out playin' with my football and I looked up an' he was watchin' me from way off in the trees. I called him to come over, but he waved, for me to go to him. When I got to where he'd been standin', he wasn' there no more, he'd gone farther away, and every time I went after him, he'd move again. Then I knowed he was leadin' me deeper and deeper into the trees. I runned home and told me ma, an' that was when she told me about him. She said he was a ghost and never to follow him again. He started comin' around all the time then. He has everyone right upset. 'Swhy we're movin'.'

'Do you know who he is?'

'My mam says he was kilt and buried in these woods. So now he can't leave.'

'Do any of your people know how to get rid of ghosts like him?'

'No. My gran tried, like I told ya, but he din't go.'

I opened the door and Millie scampered back in.

'He tole my little brother his name is Thomas,' the kid said.

'Did he?' I asked, feeling genuinely scared for the first time since all this had started.

'Yeah. My brother was in bed one night, an' he waked up and seen this face at the window. My brother was real scared, an' he tole him to go 'way. The ghost tried to get him to go out 'n' play. My brother wouldn't go, though. He knowed if he did, he wouldn't never be able to come back.'

'Did Thomas say anything else?'

'He says he's lonely, that he's not got any friends. That's what he wants, I think. A friend. He wants someone to play with *real* bad.'

44

Gerry Blaney called me early the following Wednesday morning.

'You know how I said we were quits?'

'Yes.'

'We're not. You owe me big time.'

'I don't follow.'

'As a result of sending two men out to do the little favour you requested, I am down a couple of employees!'

'What happened?' I could feel a headache coming on, and I hadn't been drinking the night before.

'Not over the phone. Come to the dealership.'

'On my way.'

∗

He was sitting in his office when I arrived, the usual tumbler of whiskey in his hand even though it was just seven forty-five in the morning.

'What did you send my lads out against?' he snapped without preamble.

'I told you. His name is Rex Gifford.'

'He's not just some thug you've fallen foul of, though, is he?'

'No.'

'He was supposed to be the one getting the scaring, but he put the wind up my lads good and proper. One of them is in hospital – he lost most of his teeth. The other is physically alright – bit of bruising – but he'll not work in the strong-arm business again. He's a nervous bloody wreck.'

'*What happened*, Gerry?'

'I sent out two of my best, I want you to know that.'

'Fair enough. Thank you.'

'It didn't take them long to find him. Did you know he's working in a bookshop in the city centre?'

I shook my head dolefully.

'I didn't, but it fits.'

'My boys went in near closing time, browsed for a while. It turned out very nicely, or so they thought, 'cause he was left to lock up, so he was there on his own. But it didn't work out nicely. Not at all.'

'He turned the tables on them.'

'Fucker must have smelled a rat, because he jumped them before they had a chance to put the squeeze on him. He walloped Hughy in the mouth with an encyclopaedia, and disabled Trevor with a kick in the goolies. When they were down, he tied them both up and locked the door of the shop.'

'Fucking hell.'

'I'm not sure what he did to them, or what he said, and they won't tell me. Suffice it to say, they are scared witless and have handed in their resignations. Trevor is even talking about moving his family out of the area. What I want to know from *you*, Sonny Jim, is who the fuck that little weasel is, and why you didn't tell me I needed to send more men?'

'He's someone who bears a grudge against me.'

'Why?'

'I sort of had him put in prison.'

'For what?'

'Does it matter?'

Gerry sniffed. 'Not really. Well, you can sleep easy – as per your instructions, my lads didn't lay a finger on him. They never had the fucking opportunity.'

45

Later that night I pulled out my old case files on Gifford. I couldn't think of anything else to do, so I thought I'd return to the source, to where it all began.

I pushed back the furniture and spread the paperwork over the floor in my living room: all the old notes and observations I had made during the investigation and then the trial. I hoped that somewhere in the midst of all the shadows of the past I might find a clue as to how to get this monster off my back and prevent him from continuing his path of destruction.

I spent three hours poring over everything I had, going through each log entry, word for word, hoping against hope that there was something I had seen back then that I hadn't known I'd seen.

The psychologist's report on Gifford told me just what it had three years ago: *extreme lack of empathy; narcissistic personality traits; IQ in the gifted range; tendencies towards violence and sadism.* I read back over the court transcripts, as I had only attended the trial on the day I was due to give evidence (I did not need to be there for the rest of it, and was already sickened by the case and longed to be done with it). To my huge surprise, I saw that Gifford had said very little when asked to take the stand, his responses bordering on the monosyllabic.

This stopped me in my tracks – Gifford was usually verbose in the extreme. Why had he denied himself the chance to perform before an attentive audience? I looked through the list of people in attendance on the day, looking for someone who might have, in some inexplicable manner, spooked this usually supremely confident man.

And there it was: a witness for the prosecution (meaning she spoke up on behalf of the victim, Hayley Porter). She had only been in court once, the day Gifford himself had been called. I looked at the name and felt the surge of an emotion I had not experienced for some time: *hope.*

The person in question was named Jessica Hayes-Gifford – she was Rex Gifford's mother.

According to the transcripts and notes, Jessica was Gifford's only surviving relative – his father had died fifteen years previously. Although now in her eighties, she was a formidable woman who still ran a large set of business interests and had advanced degrees in science, economics and industrial history. I saw that she had voluntarily contacted the Director of Public Prosecutions, coming forward after her son had been arrested and offering to speak at the trial.

Her evidence against Rex was damning in the extreme: she

stated that he had exhibited deep psychological problems from an early age, which included signs of cruelty to animals, difficulties forming relationships and violent impulses towards other children. He had been through a barrage of psychologists, several of whom resigned after only one session, stating he needed specialist help. Sexual violence began when he was ten years old: he attacked one of the maids the family employed, injuring her badly.

'We had him institutionalised after that,' Mrs Hayes-Gifford said, 'He seemed to be responding to the treatment – but I now know he was just giving the doctors the answers they wanted. He was too clever for them.'

He left home when he was twenty, having dropped out of college, and began his roving lifestyle.

'I thought he was looking for somewhere he fitted in, but it is clear he was fleeing the families of the women he hurt. I had to pay some off to prevent them pressing charges – I thought I was protecting him, but what I was really doing, and I am ashamed to say it, was colluding. He only ever came home when he needed something, and that was usually to hide behind mother's skirts, generally when he had gone too far and got himself in serious trouble. He knew that with enough money he could buy his way out of a lot. Until I cut him off, that is.'

On the fifth occasion her son presented her with a demand for money because a family was threatening him with criminal prosecution, Jessica informed him that she was writing him out of her will and ceasing all payments to him unless he sought proper psychiatric help. He refused. She made good on her threat, and that day in court was the first time the pair had set eyes on one another in ten years. She was unequivocal in her view that her son was guilty.

'I know well what my son is – a monster. He does not care who he hurts, and I believe him to be a danger to society at large, and women in particular. A custodial sentence would, I feel, be the only prudent course of action. He needs to be locked away. It hurts me to say that, but it is true. He will only continue to brutalise people unless someone stops him.'

I opened my laptop and went online. Jessica Hayes-Gifford was still alive and remained the chairperson of her company. I rang the number for its head office and left a message on the machine.

'I need to speak to Mrs Hayes-Gifford urgently,' I said. 'I want to talk to her about her son.

46

He was waiting for me outside school the next evening.

'Why, Shane, how are you?'

I pretended he wasn't there and walked on past him.

'Thanks for sending your two friends to see me. Charming blokes. Did they tell you we had a nice visit?'

I went out the school gate but did not go in the direction of home – I turned right instead and began to walk up the town. I wanted to keep in places where there were lots of people, and I had a different destination in mind.

'No? Well, I'm not surprised. I don't think Hughy *could* talk when I let him go.'

I paused, looking in the window of a shop that had men's suits in the window.

'I gather Maura has returned to the bosom of her family. Pity, really. We had some unfinished business, me and her. I was so looking forward to seeing her again and taking our relationship to the next level.'

I gritted my teeth and continued to climb the shallow hill the main street was built on. I was not going to take the bait. If anyone was going to do anything stupid, it was going to be him.

'You know, you have me all wrong, Shane. You see me as your enemy. I'm not. I wish to parley a truce with you.'

I kept walking, eyes ahead.

'I am not the aggressor here. I never was. Those girls – even your good friend Maura – they *wanted* what I did. They were all so needy, they practically begged for it! Don't you see, I never committed any crimes. I was just acting on their wishes. Remember sweet little Hayley Porter?'

I continued to put one foot in front of the other. Gifford still hadn't worked out where I was going. Good.

'I went to prison because she was too repressed to say that she got exactly what she wanted. I *knew* what her most private wishes were. Even you admitted I understood her better than most people, certainly better than you. I got through all those defences the autism had built, and found the real person.'

I could see my destination now. I picked up the pace just a bit.

'If you want me to leave you alone and put an end to all this unpleasantness, all you have to do is tell me you know I am an innocent man, a man who has been wronged and unfairly maligned. Tell me that and you need never see me again.'

I stopped. Gifford's smile faltered when he realised I had led him right to the doors of the Garshaigh police station. Mine didn't. I gave him a huge grin.

'Fuck you,' I said. 'You sick, twisted, animalistic asshole.'

Rex Gifford scowled and turned to go. 'Just remember I gave you a chance,' he said. 'When it all comes down on you, don't blame me.'

I watched him walk away and prayed it wouldn't come to that.

47

The following Monday was careers day at the school, with representatives from a wide range of professions coming in to talk to the kids about the joys, trials and tribulations of working in their chosen areas.

As my main role was as a resource teacher, I didn't have much involvement with the various talks that were taking place, and spent most of the day in a classroom preparing classes for the following week.

When I got to the staff room at one thirty to grab a late lunch, I found it empty except for a man who I did not recognise, but assumed to be one of the invited guest speakers. He appeared to be going over notes for whatever talk he was giving that afternoon, so I left him to it.

I made some tea and sat down at a table at the back of the room.

'Um … sorry to interrupt, but could you tell me where room 3B is, please?'

'Of course. You go downstairs and it's right at the end of the corridor. The numbers are on the doors, so you should find it easily enough.'

The man thanked me. 'I've never done this before – I'm seriously nervous, I'm not kiddin' ya.'

'Which group are you talking to?' I asked.

'Leaving Certs, I think.'

'You don't know which class, though?'

He pulled a tatty piece of paper from his pocket. 'LC3. That's what it says here, anyway.'

'They're a nice enough bunch. What are you talking to them about?'

'I'm a solicitor.'

'Excellent. What kind of law do you practise?'

'I've been asked to cover everything, from conveyancing to some of the stuff I do for Free Legal Aid.'

'Well, I'm sure they'll be fascinated.'

He nodded but still looked uncomfortable, standing in front of me with his bag clutched to his chest, his tie askew.

'What time are you giving the talk?' I asked.

'Two.'

'It's only twenty to now. Why don't you take a seat and relax.'

He nodded and pulled up a chair opposite me. 'I'm Barry Hemmings,' he said, thrusting his hand out to me.

We shook hands.

'How come you're so nervous?' I wondered aloud. 'As a lawyer, I thought you'd be used to talking to people, addressing groups.'

'I am. Public speaking isn't my problem. It's just that … well, I was a student here myself, and I fucking hated the place, swore I'd never come back. The only contact I've had with it since is a batshit crazy teacher I had to deal with on a case I took last year.'

'One of our teachers batshit crazy?' I laughed. 'Surely not!'

He laughed, some of the tension leaving him.

'I know I'm not supposed to ask,' I said, 'but was this teacher in trouble for something?'

'No. She came to talk to me about this kid I was representing. The young fella wasn't the brightest lightbulb in the pack, got himself in serious trouble over unpaid parking fines. She had kind of taken him under her wing, from what I could tell. He's dead now, poor little fucker.'

I felt my heart quicken a little.

'If he's dead, it's okay to talk about him, right?'

'Why're you interested?'

'This is Tim Fox?'

'How'd you know?'

'The batshit crazy teacher you mentioned asked me to look in to the circumstances of his death.'

'Why?'

'I used to do that kind of work. You were Tim's lawyer?'

'Yes. For all of about ten minutes. It was just a matter of going through the motions.'

'You must have talked to Tim, though?'

'A bit, yeah. I had a notion to try and plead that here was a kid who'd never had a decent start in life. His mam is an alco of the worst kind, never gave a shite about him. He told me his dad was a brute, the only contact he had with him when he was little was to feel his fist. Other than this Maura woman at the school here, there wasn't a teacher who cared about him, and he left without being able to write anything but his name.'

'Sounds like it might have been a convincing argument,' I said.

'I never got to make it. Kid was put on the stand and just froze. Judge thought he was being difficult. That was all she wrote.'

'Down he went.'

'That was it, yeah.'

'So here was a kid, with no real record, a neglectful background, educationally challenged, handed a custodial sentence for something as stupid as parking tickets? Surely you could have appealed it?'

'I asked Tim if he wanted to. He said no.'

'What?'

'He told me to leave it alone. You know, I think he was actually afraid of going back into court again.'

'I assure you he found prison scarier.'

'Well, he never got in contact with me again. That day in court was the last time I saw him.'

'Did you try talking to his mother?'

'The case was heard at eleven fifteen in the morning and she was already pissed. It would have been a waste of my time. Anyway all she cared about was how it all impacted on her, how she was going to be all alone. She couldn't have cared less about him.'

I had finished my sandwich by then, and my cup was empty in front of me. 'Thanks for your time,' I said. 'I'd better get back to work.'

'No problem. Hope it helped you some.'

'It actually did. You reminded me of something I had forgotten.'

'What's that?'

'That at the centre of all this was a kid.'

'I think he was twenty, legally an adult.'

'Yeah, but in most other ways he was still a child. I had lost sight of that.'

'If you say so.'

'Good luck with your talk,' I said, and went back to my classroom.

I was glad I'd met him.

48

My phone rang at ten that night, and it was Jessica Hayes-Gifford.

'You said you wanted to talk to me about my son.'

'Yes.'

'If you are looking for money you will be disappointed.'

'I don't want any money, ma'am. I want your help.'

'Oh?'

'Are you aware that Rex is out of prison?'

'Of course.'

'He raped and beat my friend nearly to death a couple of weeks ago.'

There was a long silence on the end of the phone. I waited. I was afraid she would hang up, but she didn't.

'I washed my hands of Rex many years ago. I am sorry he hurt someone you care for, but I do not see what I can do about it.'

'Your son is spiralling out of control, ma'am. He is paranoid and deluded. I know he will strike again and again until *someone* stops him. Now that might mean the police catching him, or it might mean an angry father or brother or husband seeking a different kind of restitution.'

'Rex is not so easy to subdue.'

'I know, but one day he will meet his match.'

'He is no longer my concern, Mr Dunphy. I came forward five years ago and I believe it was my testimony that had him put away for as long as he was. I think I have done my bit.'

'He has hurt one woman already – he will hurt many more unless something is done.'

She was quiet again.

'I need some time to think.'

'I'll wait for your call.'

She hung up.

49

Father Senan Malone came to the offices of *The Western News* the next day. Chaplin gave me a funny look, but excused himself and went out to get coffee, leaving the old priest and me alone to talk.

'I think I owe you an apology, son,' he said, looking at his knees as he spoke. 'I have been thinking a great deal about your visit, examining my conscience about the events that took place here all those years ago. I feel I may not have been as open with you as I could have been.'

'I'm listening,' I said.

'Winifred Tobin was a very disturbed woman.' He intoned the words slowly and deliberately, almost as if he was reciting a sermon. 'She confided in me, on more than one occasion, that she had bouts of severe melancholia, during which she thought about, even went so far as to plan, killing her son and then herself. I managed to talk her out of it, point out all the positive things she had in her life, but in truth she had very little to live for.'

'I would have thought having a child was a fairly significant reason to get up in the morning,' I said.

'I put that to her. She had it in her head that there was something wrong with the boy. She said he had his father's evil in him, that he was bad. She felt he was always watching her, she talked about him having accusatory eyes.'

'If she was depressed, you should have persuaded her to see a doctor.'

'I know that now. Things were different then, mental illness was not as well understood. Winifred was already dealing with the stigma of being an unmarried mother, I didn't want to load another taboo on her shoulders. I feared it would be too much to bear.'

'It clearly was, Father.'

'I arrived at the house one afternoon, and no one was home. I waited for a while, and saw her coming out of the woods. She loved to walk among the trees, so I was not surprised. But then I saw there was something wrong – she seemed to be staggering, unsteady. I went to meet her, and saw she had blood on her hands, on her blouse. She told me she had fallen and cut herself while she was out walking. We went inside and she cleaned herself up. The following day, she told me the boy was gone, that his father had taken him.'

'You told me before that you believed her.'

'I wanted to. But a part of me suspected, right from that moment, that she had done something terrible. When she ended her life, I even went to the police, told them what I thought. They didn't seem to care, they were convinced Thomas was a figment of a mad woman's imagination. But I knew different.'

'You're sure he was real.'

'I am.'

'And you believe she killed him.'

'God help me, I do, yes.'

I sat back and rubbed my eyes. It was the conclusion I had been slowly reaching, but to have it spoken aloud made it seem frighteningly real.

'That poor boy,' Father Malone said, his voice cracking with misery. 'He never even had a funeral. I should have gone out there and prayed for his soul, but I was too afraid.'

'You might get your chance yet,' I said. 'I don't think we've heard the last of Thomas Tobin.'

DR B: My God. She killed him.

SD: It looks that way.

DR B: Is there anything you can do about that?

SD: It had already been reported. This is a child the local population *still* refuses to believe ever existed. And to be honest, it suits them to keep thinking that. Standing by and allowing a mother to murder her child is something no community wants to own up to. Murder-suicide, or familicide, or whatever you want to call it, is alarmingly well known now, but in the eighties is was almost unheard of, a terrible scandal. I think the people of Garshaigh – and I include Father Malone in this too – dealt with it with the only resources they had at their disposal.

DR B: A mother and a little boy died and the world looked away.

SD: Yes.

DR B: But you wouldn't look away.

SD: I *couldn't*. There's a difference. I felt as if this kid was calling out to us, somehow. Like he wanted me to acknowledge what had happened. Whether I was experiencing some form of group hysteria or I was seeing some kind of feral boy who was living out in the woods or I was actually seeing a ghost, I don't know, but it looked like this terrible thing was rearing its head again and wouldn't be brushed under the carpet this time.

DR B: What goes around comes around.

50

When I got home that day Devereux's black Volvo was parked outside my house. The man himself was leaning against a lamp post and frightening the neighbours. He grinned as I extended my hand for him to shake.

'You've finally made it to the country,' I said. 'I thought you started to melt once you got as far as the suburbs.'

'Oh, I fancied a drive,' he said, following me inside. 'What the hell is this?'

Millie was standing in the hallway, eyeing us both with open disdain.

'This is Millie. She adopted me a couple of years ago.'

'I never would have figured you for the dog type.'

'I think the problem with our relationship is that Millie isn't really the person type. I was just about to make dinner, have you eaten?'

'The purpose of my visit isn't social, Shane. Goitre got back to me. I thought you'd want to hear about it right away.'

'For sure. What've you got?'

'Is she going to continue staring at us like that?'

Millie was giving Devereux a particularly penetrating look.

'Ignore her. She's prone to moodiness.'

We sat down in the kitchen.

'According to Goitre, Tim Fox was playing a very dodgy game. He was working for Wheeler Bowyers and – this surprised even me, I have to admit it – working for Ballsack at the same time.'

'Working for *Ballsack*? The same person who raped, abused and bullied him so badly we thought he might have incited him to kill himself?'

'The same.'

'That doesn't make sense on any level.'

'Actually, when you look at it from a certain perspective, it kind of does.'

'Enlighten me.'

'We know Tim was the recipient of Ballsack's amorous attentions.'

'We do. Although it seems wrong to call them that.'

'We know that Monty Drew managed to impress on Ballsack the error of his ways, as those ways applied to Tim.'

'I'm following you so far.'

'And we know that Monty made parole and was to be released. This caused him concern, as he would no longer be available to defend his young ward's honour against Ballsack and his associates.'

'Yes, all this I understand.'

'Monty told us that he employed Bob Stills, a rather fearsome gentleman, to act in his stead, and Ballsack admitted that Bob was not as conscientious in his duties as Monty might have liked him to be, but that eventually Bob did step up and sort things out, an action that involved giving the aforementioned Mister Sack a thorough hiding, while getting Tim a job with Wheeler Bowyers as an added protective measure. What Ballsack refrained from telling us is that Bob Stills also got Tim a job working for *him*. I think he was, in a twisted kind of way, trying to get Ballsack to make up for what he had done by giving Tim a position among his gang and an easy job that he would have to pay him for.'

'Doing what, for the love of God?' I asked.

'There are very few jobs one can really apply for when it comes to the prison black market. It's either prostitution or dealing drugs. Tim did not enjoy the former, so he settled for the latter.'

'Well, he did have some experience, I suppose,' I said.

'And the bad batch we've been hearing so much about? It wasn't Wheeler who brought that in – it was our good friend Brian.'

'This is getting really fucking complicated,' I said.

'It has a certain Chandleresque quality to it, alright.'

'Where do we go with this?'

'I told Ballsack I'd come looking if I had any more questions,' Devereux said. 'And I think a few posers have popped into my head.'

'I reckon I could drink some more of that coffee,' I agreed.

'Oh, Brian doesn't work at The Checker anymore,' Devereux said. 'He tried to beat one of the customers to death with a chopping board. He's back on The Shaker.'

51

I mentioned before that I don't like prisons much – I often experience something akin to a mild panic attack when around them. It doesn't always happen, though, because I have spent years trying to suppress this rising sense of claustrophobia, as my job gives me cause to spend fairly regular periods visiting correctional facilities. Unfortunately, my efforts to address this phobia have only been successful in a hit and miss kind of way, and it often resurfaces at the most inopportune times.

Salt Island is my vision of what hell might look like. Sailing out to it one first sees a black smudge on the horizon, little more than a speck, as the vastness of the ocean opens up beyond the city's sheltered harbour. As you get closer, you gradually discern the old military fort that has been adapted into the prison which exists today. I regularly find myself wondering what a prisoner who is facing a lengthy sentence must feel when he is on his way there, knowing that this gullshit-covered rock a mile from shore is going to be home for the foreseeable future.

Inside isn't much better. The term 'they don't build them like they used to' was never so apt: impossibly thick walls contain a maze of tiny cells, the narrow corridors echo with screams, magnifying the jingling keys and the patrolling footsteps of the guards into a nightmare cacophony.

The evening Devereux and I caught the ferry to Salt Island to meet Ballsack was one of those occasions when I knew I was going to have to fight hard to keep my composure, and the weather wasn't helping: as we got closer to the city, dark clouds began to gather overhead and the wind started to develop a threatening timbre.

'Is this a good idea?' I asked.

'Getting cold feet?'

'It looks as if we're both going to get wet feet.'

By the time we reached the dock the rain was coming in sheets and the water was grey and choppy.

'The forecast says it's going to get a whole lot worse as the night goes on,' the boat's pilot said. We were joined on the crossing by the next team of prison staff, going over for the night-time shift. 'They don't need to get back until morning, but I expect you'd like to.'

'We shouldn't be terribly long,' I said, feeling a bit green about the gills as the small boat dipped and bobbed – and we hadn't even cast off yet.

'I'll give you three quarters of an hour, then I'm off,' the pilot said. 'I'm paid to get staff on and off the island, and I can't do that if I'm stuck out there waiting for you pair to do whatever errand of mercy you're on.'

I threw up twice on the way over; my stomach, already a knot of tension at the thoughts of permitting myself to be locked into The Shaker, felt like it was also being put through the spin cycle of a particularly enthusiastic washing machine. Devereux stood, calm and impassive as ever, and held onto my belt as I leaned over the side to vomit up what was left in my stomach. I was glad we hadn't stopped for dinner.

By the time we landed it was blowing a proper gale and the rain was peppered with chunks of ice and hail.

'Forty-five minutes!' the pilot barked as we bent forward into the wind and made our way up the slippery concrete steps to the prison.

There are three stages a visitor has to go through to gain entry to Salt Island: it begins in a kind of holding area, a little like a dentist's waiting room, except there is a huge metal door set into the wall, looming over you like a cyclopean eye. After this comes a security check, where your belongings are passed through a metal detector, and a guard and his sniffer dog give you the once over in a bid to detect drugs and other contraband. Finally, there is a room I like to think of as 'the scanner' – a windowless, coffin-like chamber where a red light goes up and down over the occupants, presumably to ensure you haven't smuggled in anything internally.

By the time we got to the visiting area, I was white as a ghost and drenched in sweat. The whole entry process had taken fifteen minutes. Time had become extremely important to me, now I knew we were on such a tight deadline.

I just hoped Ballsack was going to be accommodating and brief.

It became immediately evident that he had other intentions.

'Not you pair again. I've nothin' more to say to yiz.'

'Yet here you are,' Devereux said. 'You didn't have to agree to see us.'

'I'm bored. I think you're funny. Especially him.' He motioned at me. 'Hey, Slick. You don't look so well.'

'Yet still he looks better than you,' Devereux said. 'Why did you not share the fact that Tim Fox was working for you?'

'Who says he was?'

'People who know such things and are more reliable than you are.'

'Look, he might have done one or two things for me now and again – I would've thought you'd be fuckin' happy I was bein' nice to him.'

I could hear the sea booming and crashing outside, even through the six-foot-thick walls of the Victorian building. Every pound was like a fist hitting me between the shoulder blades.

'Why'd you employ him?' I asked, trying to keep my mind focused on the conversation and not on the sound of the door being locked and bolted behind us by the guard who had shown us in.

'Bob Stills asked me to. When Bobby asks you for somethin', you don't fuckin' argue.'

'And no one saw it as a conflict of interest, seeing as Tim was also working as a runner for Wheeler Bowyers?'

'Why would they? It's a free fuckin' market economy in here, isn't it?'

'I doubt Wheeler would see it that way.'

'Are you gonna tell him?' Ballsack leaned in threateningly.

Devereux didn't say a word. He just held the man's gaze, his expression, to me at least, appearing completely neutral. Ballsack saw something else, though, because he pulled back and looked apologetic. 'I was just tryin' to keep everyone fuckin' happy is all.'

'Well, I am far from happy, Brian.'

'Don't call me that. No one fuckin' calls me that!'

'The materials Tim was moving for you – how did you get them inside?'

'Do you think I am a fuckin' retard or somethin'? I'm not tellin' youse that!'

'Okay. Let me rephrase. The product you were selling was basically poison. We know this. Was it your drugs that killed Tim?'

'Fuck off, will ya? Keep your voice down!'

'Neither the prison guards nor the police are interested in pursuing this case, Brian,' Devereux said. 'The book is closed on it as far as anyone other than Shane and myself are concerned. We just want to know the truth so we can tell a lady who actually gave a damn about this young man's life that he did not die at his own hand due to fear and misery. Knowing it was a stupid accident and he was dead before he had a chance to suffer will put her mind at ease.'

'Yeah, well, maybe,' Ballsack muttered.

'What was that?' Devereux asked.

'Maybe that's what happened,' Ballsack said, a little louder this time.

We were the only people in the visitors' room. No one else was mad enough to come out on such a foul night, and the guard at the door was watching *Coronation Street* on the TV attached to the wall above the door. We were at the other end of the room, and he didn't seem concerned about what we were talking about. It was as private as a prison is likely to get.

'What happened, Brian?' Devereux hissed, grabbing Ballsack's arm in a grip that made the big man wince in pain.

'It wasn't meant to happen, alright?' he said, spitting out the words.

'What wasn't?'

'He was only meant to take a small bit, just to see if it was okay.'

I felt as if a hole had opened beneath me and I was tumbling in. I had to hold on to the desk in front of me for fear I might actually slide on to the floor. 'Are you saying what I think you're saying?' I asked, unable to keep the incredulity from my voice.

'I fuckin' told him to only do, like, a small amount, and to inject it between his toes. I thought that'd be safer. I gave him a small chunk and told him to just break off a tiny bit, cook it down and do a hit. He was to let us know what the buzz was like, you get what I'm sayin'? I didn't want it goin' out until we were sure it wasn't gonna bring no shit down on us. But the stupid little fucker did the whole lot. How was I to know he was such a dope?'

'You used him as a guinea pig,' I said, still finding it hard to process. 'You tested out that poison on Tim, knowing it was probably lethal.'

'Slow down now, Slick. There was no way to be sure what it was until someone tried it. He fuckin' offered!'

'He was twenty years old,' I said, not able to contain my anger any more. 'He was barely more than a kid, for fuck sake. You beat him, you raped him, and then you killed him. I hope you're happy, you brutish, disgusting lout of a man.'

'You better watch how you talk to me, pal,' Ballsack said darkly.

'If you move so much as a centimetre, Brian, I will break your eye socket,' Devereux said conversationally.

'Why couldn't you just have left him alone?' I said, barely aware of anything other than the sense of complete, sickening injustice.

'Life ain't like that,' Ballsack said.

'Well it fucking should be,' I said in disgust, and standing up, walked to the door, where the guard let me out, his eyes never leaving the TV.

I met our pilot in the waiting area.

'We're not going anywhere for a while,' he said. 'Hope you brought a sleeping bag.'

I said nothing, just sat down on one of the seats, too tired and sick to care.

Devereux came out fifteen minutes later. He sat down next to me. 'I have agreed we will not tell the authorities anything we learned this evening,' he said.

'I didn't.'

'That is true. Brian will deny every word, though. It's all hearsay.'

I sighed deeply and looked out the window as a massive wave broke across the rocks outside, completely covering one block of the jail for several long seconds.

'You gonna tell Goitre?'

'I might just do that,' Devereux said.

'Will that make things difficult for Ballsack?'

'Well, it won't make things easier for him, that's for sure.'

We sat in that little room, trying to sleep on the uncomfortable chairs, until six the following morning, when the weather finally broke.

I remember awaking around three to see Devereux standing at the glass, looking out at the storm, and for the first time in all the years I had known him I thought he looked incredibly sad and lonely, as if the weight of all the anguish and horror he had seen was heavy upon him.

I wanted to say something, but at that moment the gulf between us seemed too great, and I closed my eyes and pretended to sleep while my friend gazed at the cruel sea, until dawn came and carried us away from that awful place.

DR B: So you saw a side of him you hadn't seen before.

SD: I did.

DR B: A more human side. When you speak of him, you often portray him as this invulnerable superhero type. In that moment, you saw that he wasn't. He's as lost and frightened as the rest of us.

SD: Perhaps.

DR B: Do you think any less of him for having seen that vulnerability?

SD: No! Why would I?

DR B: Yet you were too embarrassed to reach out to him, to say anything.

SD: *I* wasn't embarrassed. I thought *he* might be.

DR B: Why?

SD: We don't have that kind of relationship.

DR B: But you call on him to help when you're out of your depth; he confides in you, telling you things that must be quite personal to him, like his experience of being tortured – why not ask him if he's okay when he obviously needed some comfort?

SD: I just thought it would be an infringement of the boundaries
        Karl has spent a long time building. I don't think he would
        want me to see him as anything other than what he presents.

DR B: Once again, a very simplistic view.

SD: We'll have to agree to disagree on that one.

52

I got home at eight that morning to find Fred Stubbs, the man whose daughter Gifford had approached in a café in Limerick what felt like a lifetime ago, standing at my front door. He looked as if he had been crying, which was something of a coincidence, as I felt a bit like crying myself.

'He attacked her,' was all he said.

'I'm sorry,' I said helplessly.

And then he did break down.

The bookshop was just where Gerry Blaney said it was. It was one of those stores that was faux olde worlde – all stressed wood and artfully peeling paint. Gifford and another assistant, a studious-looking young man, were just opening as I arrived. I followed them in.

'Shane, so glad you could come,' he said, but I cut across him.

'You dumb fuck!'

The assistant looked at me in shock, then grabbed a clipboard and hurried to the other end of the shop.

'Calm down, now,' Gifford said, making shushing movements with his hands.

'I'm perfectly calm, Rex,' I said, laughing manically. 'I'm calm because the moment has finally arrived! I knew it would come around eventually, and it has. You think you're some kind of genius, and I don't doubt you're clever in a lot of ways, but you've fucked up good and proper now.'

'What are you talking about?'

He didn't seem sure of himself, just then. Maybe it was the fact that I had thrown caution to the wind, perhaps it was because I sounded more than a little deranged, or it could have been that I seemed so convinced of what I was saying, but I heard doubt in his voice.

'You have attacked the daughter of a newspaper editor. And he's really pissed off. Now, let me be clear, Rex – he isn't a sub-editor and he isn't the features editor. He runs the whole motherfucking show. He has the last say on what goes into each and every column. Writes a few himself. In next week's paper, guess who is on the front page?'

I raised my phone and snapped a photo of him before he could stop me.

'He asked me to get a shot of you to accompany the piece. I'm writing a section about your past history to go in it as well. It's important to be thorough, don't you agree?'

'You can't do that,' he said, no fun or jollity in his voice now. He was angry. Scared.

'Yes we can.'

'I'll sue you. Ruin you both.'

I laughed. Hysterically. A few people had come into the shop by then, and they looked at us both cautiously before moving as far away as they could.

'You beat the shit out of Fred's daughter, Rex. I don't know why you didn't rape her too. But you have made a huge mistake – he's beside himself with anger, and he doesn't care if you sue him. By the time you do, the paper will be out and everyone will have read it. Your name will be mud. They might publish a retraction but by then it will be too late. People don't read retractions, Rex. They'll fucking read a great big front-page story about a serial sex offender who is living right slap bang in the middle of them, though. You stupid, dumb pervert. You've only gone and done yourself over.'

He hit me so hard I was lifted right off my feet. He was a little man, but by God he could throw a punch. Bells rang, galaxies soared before my eyes, and I landed with a thud flat on my back, all the wind knocked out of my lungs.

I think I was out for a moment, but awareness gradually shimmered back to me and I painfully began to gather myself. Propping myself up on an elbow, I saw a man trying to restrain Gifford and a young couple, probably students, standing to one side, looking worried. The boy came over and helped me to my feet.

'You should leave now,' he said. 'He still seems pretty mad.'

I rubbed my jaw, which hurt like hell. 'I'm going,' I said. Then to Gifford: 'But I'll be back. See, this time, I have witnesses.'

53

When I got back to my car I rang the police, stating what had happened and pointing out in the strongest possible terms that Gifford was in breach of parole. Earlier I had begged Stubbs to impress upon his daughter the need to file a complaint, although, when he had calmed down enough to speak sensibly, he told me she had been attacked from behind as she walked home from college, and would not in all likelihood be a particularly reliable witness.

I agreed to call to the station to make a statement on my way to work (for which I was already late), and then pointed my car towards Garshaigh.

I was sick from lack of sleep, my nerves buzzed with tension and my head ached from the thump I had just received, but I still felt as if a weight had been lifted from my shoulders – the people who had been in the store would all report that I had acted like a madman, but there was no denying a blow had been struck and it had not come from me. That meant one thing and one thing only: Rex Gifford was going back to prison. It wasn't the way I had wanted to achieve my goal, but it was a result.

I was halfway home when my phone rang, Orla Finnegan's number flashing on the screen.

'Hey, Orla.'

'He's gone.'

She sounded on the verge of breaking, her voice had that edge to it.

'Slow down and tell me what happened.'

'He came for him. I saw the boy, Thomas, this time.'

'He was in the house?'

'Standing in the kitchen. We were eating breakfast and I left the back door open to bring some rubbish out to the bins. I came back and he was there, holding Gregory by the hand. I screamed and went to grab him, but they ran right past me like I wasn't there. I tried to catch them … I don't know how they moved so *fast*.'

'Do you know where they went?'

'Into the woods. Where they always go.'

'Okay. I'm on my way. Have you called the police?'

'What would I tell them, that he went out to play? He's only gone an hour or so. I'm scared, Shane. That boy looked so strange.'

I called George Taylor and told him what had happened.

'I have a school to run, Shane, and while we're on that subject, I don't pay you to roam the countryside looking for wayward children.'

'George, this isn't your usual runaway. There's something very weird going on. You know the woods better than anyone. I need your help.'

'I don't think I can be of assistance. It would not be appropriate for me to desert my post.'

'Fair enough. Thanks anyway.'

I stopped off to pick up Millie. She knew Gregory's scent and while she was not a hunting dog, I figured she might lead me to him – Millie didn't like many people, but she did seem to have taken a shine to Gregory. And she could act as an early warning sign if Thomas was nearby – she seemed terrified of him.

When I got to the Finnegans' I was surprised to see George Taylor's car parked out front after all, with its owner, dressed for a hike, leaning against the bonnet.

'I thought you were afraid you might be charged with dereliction of duty,' I said.

'I'd never be able to live with myself if anything happened to the boy.'

I got one of Gregory's old socks from Orla, so Millie would have something to work with.

'I've had a look about,' George said. 'They didn't leave us much to go on, but from what tracks there are, it seems they're heading north, towards the mountains.'

'I'm coming too,' Orla said.

'We're going to be travelling very quickly over rough ground,' George said to her gently. 'You don't have the footwear or the experience. And what if he came home while you were away? We'll call you occasionally to let you know how we're doing – hopefully we'll have coverage from time to time. And obviously, if he does come home, you give us a call and let us know.'

She tried to argue with us, but George would hear none of it, and eventually we set off.

George led the way at a pace just short of a run, with Millie ranging here and there, seemingly on the trail of something. Every now and then we paused to examine some markings or to consider how the land rose and fell. An hour later, we found the first definite evidence of their passage.

'Most people will naturally follow the easiest route,' George said. 'From what I can see, the two boys are doing just that. Look.'

In a patch of damp earth beside a small stream we could clearly see two distinct sets of tracks, one slightly bigger than the other.

'They crossed over here and continued northwest.'

'Can you tell how long ago they passed this way?' I asked.

'I am not an Indian tracker,' George said. 'I have a little woodcraft gleaned from years of hiking, but my skills are fairly limited.'

'Okay, Hawkeye,' I said. 'Just thought I'd ask.'

Millie, who was about a hundred yards ahead of us, made a yelping sound and skittered about excitedly, urging us forward.

'She seems to be on to something,' George said.

About midday we came to a part of the wood I recognised – I could hear the sea, and as we descended a shallow incline, I realised we were close to the old ruined shack where George and I had had our picnic lunch all those months ago. Millie had stopped dead, looking intently into a patch of undergrowth, on point. George reached into the scrub, retrieving what looked to be a piece of damp material – it was a child's glove. He held it up for Millie to sniff and she whined and yowled.

'That means either it belongs to Gregory, or someone recently soaked it in beef gravy,' I said.

We had gone fifty yards when I looked behind and saw that Millie wasn't budging – she was standing stock still exactly where she had been, ears and tail erect, like she was waiting for something. Suddenly a plaintive cry echoed through the trees. It sounded like someone – or some*thing* – in abject pain and misery.

'Tell me you heard that,' I said.

'Unfortunately I did.'

The cry came again.

'What *is* that?' I asked breathlessly as we jogged onwards.

'If I didn't know any better, I'd say it sounded like a very young child,' George said.

'But the kids we're following are eight and ten,' I said. 'That sounds like a baby.'

'Foxes can sound like that,' George said. 'So can feral cats.'

'Yet neither species makes those kinds of cries during the day,' I pointed out.

We heard the wail again and now it seemed like it came from just ahead of us.

'Whatever it is, I'm not ashamed to say it's scaring the bejesus out of me,' George muttered, but didn't falter in his steps.

And then we found him.

We crested a hillock and there was Gregory, sitting with his back against the wall of the old woodcutter's hut (or whatever it was), inexplicably fast asleep. For a second I was disoriented, as it felt like we had come at this clearing from an angle that should not have brought us there at all, but I shoved the feeling aside and knelt beside the boy. He opened his eyes.

'Where's Thomas?' he asked.

'I don't know, Greg,' I said. 'Are you okay?'

'Yeah, I'm fine. I want to go home, now.'

Millie scampered up, first licking Gregory on the face and then tugging at my sleeve with her teeth.

'Shane, we have company,' George said.

The small figure of a child was standing watching us from among the trees. He was dressed in the same anorak and jeans he had worn before, the hood drawn up and only the slightest hint of pale face visible in its shadow.

'Will you take Gregory and start walking back?' I said.

'What are you going to do?' George asked.

'I'm going to try and talk to him. I can't just leave a child alone in the woods.'

The cry sounded again – this time it was deafeningly loud.

'We don't know that what we're seeing *is* a child,' George said.

I looked again. The figure seemed closer. 'I can't take that chance.'

'I don't like this, Shane. I'm frightened and I think we all – you, me, Gregory and Millie – need to leave this place and get back to civilisation.'

'I can't,' I said.

The boy was now almost at the edge of the clearing (neither of us had seen him move), and I could make out huge black eyes in a deathly white visage.

'Thomas,' I said loudly, my heart pounding in my chest. I was absolutely terrified, but a kind of firewall had come down, and I was working on autopilot. 'Is there someone we can call? Anyone I can get to come and take you home?'

The wailing became a cacophony, drowning out all other sounds. Gregory covered his ears and I saw George wince. I stood up.

'I'm coming over, Thomas,' I shouted over the ruckus. 'I think it's time we had a chat, you and I.'

I made first one step, then another. It felt as if I were wading through treacle, each motion a huge effort. The noise was deafening, a furious caterwauling that seemed to come from everywhere and nowhere. I was so close to the boy now, I might have reached out and touched him. I got a powerful smell of earth and could see cobwebs on the sleeves of his coat and mildew and moss on the knees of his trousers.

I'm not sure what happened next. I saw a look of bewilderment spread across the spectral face, and then it looked as if something had caught Thomas by the waist with tremendous force, and in a flurry of motion he shot back through the trees, like a cartoon figure in fast forward. In a second he was gone, the screeching cries dwindling to nothing as the tiny form vanished into the forest.

'What just happened?' George asked, deadpan. 'Am I losing my mind, because what I just saw isn't possible.'

'I don't know what we saw,' I said. 'Let's just get out of here.'

I lifted Gregory and put him on my shoulders, and we began the hike back.

'Is Thomas gone now?' the boy asked.

'It looks like he is for now, Greg,' I said. 'But I think we need to do something to make sure he stays gone this time.'

DR B: Quite incredible.

SD: Do you think?

DR B: I don't know what to think. It's unlike anything I've ever heard before.

SD: Am I mad, Doctor?

DR B: You say that Gregory, George Taylor, the Travellers you met, and numerous others if the ghost stories from hikers are anything to go by, have reported seeing this boy. I could try to explain it away, and let you walk out of here thinking it was all the collective unconscious playing tricks, or that you were inhaling noxious gases being released by the wet soil in that part of the wood – but why bother? I think it is fair to say that you had an experience and it was real for you, and that is what counts.

SD: Do you believe me?

DR B: I believe you saw something. I believe you believe it. I know children, particularly in early adolescence, under laboratory conditions who have caused things to happen that is often referred to as psychokinesis. But like I said, this is all a waste of time. What do *you* think happened? That's the important thing.

SD: I think I encountered a very unhappy little boy. At the end of the day, that is what Thomas was, and what he was trying to say to us – he was desperately trying to express that he was lonely and abandoned and terribly sad.

DR B: Maybe, when you reached out to him, he couldn't cope with the fact that finally someone had heard him, and that was why he drew back.

SD: I think so too.

DR B: It's all very tragic, isn't it?

SD: I'm learning that life – and death – often is.

54

'Shane, I'm really sorry, but we have been unable to locate Rex Gifford,' Harry Doyle said to me when I finally reached the garda station later that evening.

'I don't follow,' I said.

'He went out to do the usual morning coffee run for the bookshop where he works and didn't return. We checked his address and he isn't there. No one knows where he might be. We've asked his employers and his landlord to contact us if he does show up, but for now, I regret to say, we have nothing to go on.'

'Can't you put, like, an APB out on him or anything?'

'You watch too much TV, Shane,' Harry said. 'We aren't going to put out any kind of a bulletin on some guy for popping you one. From what I've been told, you deserved it. According to the rules of his parole, if he doesn't check in with the probation services within two weeks, he'll be considered to have absconded, and we'll go looking for him then.'

'He attacked the Stubbs girl.'

'And I spoke to her. She could not give us a description of her attacker.'

'It was Rex Gifford.'

'It probably was, but I can't work with that,' Harry said. 'Now go home. You look like you're fit to collapse.'

He was right. I stood to go.

'He hit me. You have witnesses. I *am* pressing charges. So when he surfaces, I want him brought in, Harry.'

'I hear you.'

'Thank you. Now I am going home to sleep for the next six months.'

A long black car was parked at the gate of the station when I got outside. As I passed, a window rolled down.

'Mr Dunphy?'

A grey-haired elderly woman peered out at me.

'Yes.'

'I am Jessica Hayes-Gifford.'

I looked closely at the face – she had a very expensive haircut and was wearing black pearls around her neck. Could I see Rex in her? I wasn't sure. 'Your son seems to have done a bunk,' I said.

'No, he has not,' she said dryly. 'I have him.'

I tried to peer around her. 'Where?'

'Somewhere he can do no harm.'

I saw red then. The fear, frustration and anger of the past few days bubbled up and I let rip. 'He has already done terrible harm, Mrs Gifford,' I seethed. 'If you have him, hand him over to the authorities so we can have him put where he belongs, behind fucking bars! You have no right to hide him from the police. I want him locked away for what he has done, d'you hear me?'

'I do. There are many ways to bring about the conclusion you desire, so long as you can pay for the privilege,' the old woman said. 'You asked for my help. I have given it. I promise you, you will never hear from Rex again. I bid you good evening.'

The window rolled up, and the car pulled away from the kerb. I went back inside and told Harry what had happened, but he just shrugged.

'If he doesn't sign in with probation services in two weeks, then we'll have a problem,' he said.

I went home and slept for fourteen hours straight.

55

I stood with Father Malone, Orla, George Taylor, Aongus and Gregory in the woods just beyond the little house where so many strange things had happened. Millie sat watching us from the garden. It seemed that her experiences in the forest had turned her off the great outdoors for a while.

The old priest intoned the words of a blessing, asking for the soul of Thomas Tobin to be put to rest and accepted into the great beyond. I thought Father Malone deserved closure as much as anyone. When he had completed his incantations Gregory and Aongus produced candles from their pockets, and Orla lit them with a plastic lighter.

'You needs to go now, Thomas,' Gregory said. 'I liked bein' your friend, but I think you needs to go and be with your mam. You'll be happier with her.'

The two boys walked a little way into the woods and stuck their candles into the earth, then came back and joined us. We watched the flames until a gust of wind blew them both out.

'May his soul, and the souls of the faithful departed, rest in peace,' Father Malone said.

'Amen,' we all chorused, including myself, even though I wasn't religious.

In the distance, almost beyond our eyeline, I thought I saw a glimmer of movement. I looked at Gregory, and he was smiling. I think he saw it too.

'Let's go back to the house and have some tea and those cakes Father Malone brought us,' Orla said.

We had a wonderful party.

56

A month later I met Maura Bellamy to go for lunch in Dublin. The bruises had healed and she seemed happier and easier in herself, although I could sense the undercurrent of fear and hurt that was just below the surface – it would take her a long time to get over what she had been through.

'Rex Gifford is in a secure psychiatric facility in the UK,' I told her as we sat down in a very nice restaurant.

'Which his mother organised,' Maura said.

'It's all been cleared by the courts – from what I can see, they're more than happy to hand the problem over to someone else,' I said. 'His mother sent an in-depth psychiatric assessment to his probation officer, explaining that he had come to her in the throes of a serious breakdown, probably brought on by the stress of keeping his baser desires in check now that he was a free man. The report recommended a course of treatment only offered by a privately run facility in Scotland.'

'Won't he be released eventually, though?' Maura asked as the waiter brought us our starters – soup for her and potted shrimp for me.

'Mrs Hayes-Gifford assures me that he will never be a risk to anyone again. She knows what he is, and, while *she* may not be long for this world, her money will pay for his bed and board in that unit for many years to come. I think we can rest easy.'

We ate in silence for a while.

'I want to thank you for what you did for Tim,' she said.

'It was mostly down to a friend of mine actually,' I said. 'I'll pass on your appreciation.'

'It was still an awfully sad death,' Maura said – I had told her about everything we had learned about Tim, and she was still processing it. 'But at least it wasn't suicide like I had thought. And I know he suffered – that awful man who abused him … I don't know. Are we really any better off? Thank you for trying, anyway.'

'The more I got to know Tim Fox, the more I realised just how sad and lonely a kid he was,' I said. 'But the one thing he had going for him was you, Maura. He knew you cared. And while you couldn't stop him from ending up in prison, and you couldn't make him say no to drugs, I like to think that you still made a difference.'

'How?'

'In his darkest moments, he could look into his heart and know *someone* gave a damn. In my experience, that means a lot to kids like Tim.'

'I hope so.'

They brought our main courses.

'Will we have some wine?' Maura asked.

'Ms Bellamy, I do declare you are trying to lead me astray!'

'Is it terribly decadent to drink wine at lunchtime?'

'Probably. Do you want red or white?'

'White, I think.'

We sipped wine and shared stories about teaching and about life.

'Will you come back to Garshaigh?' I asked over coffee.

'I don't know. I'm terrified of what people will say.'

'They'll say: *Welcome back, Maura. It's great to see you again!*'

'Will they?'

'I think so.'

'I want to. I miss the children. I miss George and the other teachers.'

'Come back, then.'

'Maybe next September – the new academic year. It'll give me time to … to sort everything out in my head. As best I can, anyway.'

We walked up Dame Street in the early afternoon.

'I don't think I can ever forget what he did to me,' Maura said after a time.

'I don't expect you will. But you'll get used to it. It'll become a part of you, and it won't hurt so much anymore.'

'How do you know?'

'I just do.'

'It scares me to know someone like him can be real. I thought something like that would never happen to me.'

'I wish that were true.'

We reached the end of Grafton Street.

'This is where I get my bus,' I said.

'Yes.'

'You going to be okay?'

'Things are very good between me and Dad. It's one positive that has come out of all this. I don't think we'd have ever sorted out our differences if … well, if what happened hadn't happened.'

'I'm really pleased you're getting on well, Maura.'

'You take care. Call me soon.'

She hugged me tight and then turned and walked away. I watched her go, a woman who had lived through a terrible darkness and come out the other side scarred, but stronger, somehow.

'If he ever does come back, we'll be waiting,' I said gently, and turned to face the approaching evening.

Transcript of audio recording from the files of Doctor Bernadette Browne – therapy session #1 with Shane Dunphy, 30th January 2013.

SD: So, what do you think?

DR B: About what?

SD: Am I crazy?

DR B: I think you've had an exceptionally traumatic few months, but I don't believe you're suffering from any psychiatric disorder, no. If I had to make a suggestion or offer any advice, I think you need to learn to say no to people once in a while, or even suggest others who might help out instead – you are not a one-man crusade against society's ills. Can I propose you take a little time off? Do some of that walking you like, although possibly not in the woods.

SD: I might do that.

DR B: And is Rex Gifford really gone? You didn't just tell Maura that to put her mind at ease?

SD: He's a tricky little bastard, Doctor, if you'll pardon my French. I'll be looking over my shoulder for a while to come, but there is no need to bother Maura with that. She deserves a little happiness.

DR B: As do you. Perhaps you should allow yourself to have some.

SD: That'd be nice.

DR B: You are trying to evade. Are you going to be more careful, look after yourself better, take some time to process what *you* have been through?

SD: I'll certainly think about it.

DR B: Still not good enough.

SD: You are one tough lady.

DR B: Would you consider coming here again? You could let me help you to deal with some of the things that seem to be driving you. I think we've touched on them here, but I don't believe we have come to any firm conclusions at all.

SD: I'm not sure I want to know what drives me.

DR B: Then why did you come here in the first place? Why tell me all this if you didn't want to wrest some meaning from it?

SD: Who says it has any meaning? The world is a messed-up place; bad things happen to good people and bad things happen to bad people. That is the only meaning I have ever gleaned.

DR B: Yet still you try to do battle with it all, the knight errant riding in to save the day, to keep the monsters at bay and rescue all those whom no one else has even noticed are in trouble. If there is nothing but random bad luck, why bother?

(*There is a pause.*)

SD: Because I don't know how to do anything else.

DR B: Maybe we can teach you some new ways of doing things.

SD: I should warn you, I'm a notoriously bad student.

DR B: Well, luckily, I'm an excellent teacher.

(*Another pause.*)

DR B: Time's up. How are you feeling?

SD: Optimistic.

DR B: I think that's a really good start.

Afterword

My last book, *The Girl from Yesterday*, was about grief. *The Boy They Tried To Hide* follows on from that and addresses the fact that, in my experience, life is circular: we owe a debt to those who have gone before, and our actions often come back to haunt us, in many different ways.

The story of Gregory and Thomas is one I often ponder. What really happened and what I really saw are questions to which I have no answers. I have written in several of my books, now, about experiences I have had while working with children that could be described as paranormal, but I am loath to accept that labelling. Children are incredibly open beings; they take what they see at face value and are undeterred when something does not fit the bounds of scientific explanation. Maybe by working with them the way I do, and entering their world on their terms, I have been touched by that openness too.

After our candlelit ceremony, Gregory and his family were never bothered by Thomas again. Maybe all he wanted was an acknowledgement that he had been, and that his life had ended long before it should have. Sometimes that is enough.

Maura Bellamy returned to work. She told me that she spent a lot of hours in therapy and shed many tears, and finally feels she has put the horrors of Rex Gifford behind her. Her relationship with her father is stronger than ever, and she is happy and content in her life and her work. She told me that she has a picture of Tim Fox on the desk in her office at work as a reminder that every single student deserves the best effort she can give, and that no one should ever be given up on.

I know Karl Devereux would agree with her on that.

I never heard from Rex Gifford again. I often wonder if he is still 'receiving treatment' in that facility in Scotland. I hope so. The world is a safer place with him out of circulation. His mother died three years after the events described in this book, but she left a well-stocked fund to continue to pay for her son's treatment and upkeep.

Occasionally I think I see him among a crowd on a city street, but when I look a second time, he is gone. Once I was sure I spied him in a supermarket, and froze with fear until I realised I had made a mistake.

And sometimes I dream of him and wake up in a cold sweat.

They say that closure is good for the soul, and maybe it is, if you can find it.